P9-AFZ-443

DATE DUE

Dec 18			

DEMCO 38-296

A Macro Perspective
on Technology Transfer

A Macro Perspective on Technology Transfer

Allan C. Reddy

QUORUM BOOKS
Westport, Connecticut • London

Riverside Community College
MAY '97   Library
4800 Magnolia Avenue
Riverside, California 92506

T 173.3 .R43 1996

Reddy, Allan C.

A macro perspective on
  technology transfer

Library of Congress Cataloging-in-Publication Data

Reddy, Allan C.
    A macro perspective on technology transfer / Allan C. Reddy.
      p. cm.
    Includes bibliographical references and index.
    ISBN 0–89930–977–1 (alk. paper)
    1. Technology transfer. I. Title.
  T173.3.R43   1996
    338.9'26—dc20   95–51413

British Library Cataloguing in Publication Data is available.

Copyright © 1996 by Allan C. Reddy

All rights reserved. No portion of this book may be
reproduced, by any process or technique, without
the express written consent of the publisher.

Library of Congress Catalog Card Number: 95–51413
ISBN: 0–89930–977–1

First published in 1996

Quorum Books, 88 Post Road West, Westport, CT 06881
An imprint of Greenwood Publishing Group, Inc.

Printed in the United States of America

The paper used in this book complies with the
Permanent Paper Standard issued by the National
Information Standards Organization (Z39.48–1984).

10 9 8 7 6 5 4 3 2 1

This book is dedicated to my wife, Sulochana,
and to my daughters, Aparna, Anjana, and Arathi,
for their patience and understanding while
I was writing this book.

Contents

Figures and Tables

Preface

This book uses a macro approach to study the technology transfer issues. Technology can be the key to economic success for many developing countries. This is proven by the phenomenal economic success of the newly industrialized countries (NICs) of Southeast Asia (Hong Kong, Singapore, South Korea, and Taiwan) that have borrowed, adapted, and assimilated various kinds of technologies to reshape their economic systems. As a result, those nations that were once poor now claim to have become rich. Therefore, other aspiring and developing countries should emulate those that have become economically successful within a short time. Not only is using technology important; successful assimilation of newer technologies into their socioeconomic and cultural framework is also very important.

Appropriate technologies must be transferred from one nation to another without barriers. Philosophically, in the interests of general welfare, it is also the moral responsibility of the developed nations to help improve living conditions in the less developed countries (LDCs) by creating and transferring needed technologies to them. Multinational corporations (MNCs) play a crucial role in technology transfers as they transfer their proprietary technologies from one branch to another located in a different country. For example, firms like IBM transfer their manufacturing and marketing technology to their subsidiaries in other countries.

A caution about technology transfer: Technology is a double-edged sword. It can be used for constructive purposes like economic development, improving living conditions, and better health care, or it can be used to manufacture destructive weapons and to declare war on other countries. Some argue that technology has brought humankind many negative effects, including stress-related diseases caused by people's inability to cope with a world that is moving too fast due to rapid technological progress. Our interest here is to promote positive aspects of technology and technology transfer where both donors and recipients benefit.

New technology is a product of long-term investment in research and development (R&D). Thus, over time, the United States and other developed countries have invested vast sums of money in R&D in many fields to achieve their technologically superior status. The United States has reached high levels of sophistication in industrial, space, health care, and defense fields, to mention a few. Therefore, the United States is in a leadership position to organize and disseminate technologies to other countries, including the LDCs.

OBJECTIVES OF THE BOOK

A major purpose of this book is to recommend systematic approaches to transfer commercial and consumer product manufacturing and marketing technologies to LDCs. By speeding up the technology transfer and assimilation process, it is expected that general living standards will improve significantly worldwide. It is important for LDCs, including the emerging economies of the former Soviet Union, to have the right type of technologies and build their economic base quickly. Furthermore, appropriate mechanisms need to be created to assimilate transferred technologies into recipient nations in the most effective way possible.

TARGET AUDIENCE

This book is targeted to scholars, executives, policy makers, and the public. It provides guidelines to what needs to be done, and how, regarding technology transfer to developing countries. Many thought-provoking ideas and suggestions are presented.

ORGANIZATION OF THE BOOK

The book is organized as follows. Chapter 1 introduces the concepts related to technology transfer. Chapter 2 discusses the major players. Chapter 3 presents the barriers and solutions. Chapter 4 presents the ethical dimensions. Chapter 5 presents the technology transfer assimilation model. Chapter 6 discusses the application of the model to a developing country like India. Chapter 7 provides conclusions. Appendix A presents additional material on the need for and methods of transferring technology to developing countries. Appendix B furnishes the potential costs of the transfer to developing countries. Appendix C presents a model of reciprocal distribution that may have mutual benefit to the donor and recipient in the transfer process. There is a wide selection of references listed in the bibliography.

Acknowledgments

Writing a book requires the support and encouragement of many people. I am grateful to Eric Valentine, publisher of Quorum Books, for giving me the opportunity. I thank Dr. Hugh C. Bailey, President, Dr. Kenneth L. Stanley, Dean, College of Business Administration, and Dr. John E. Oliver, Jr., Chair of Management and M.I.S. and Acting Chair of the Marketing and Economics Department at Valdosta State University, for their encouragement. I am also deeply indebted to colleagues who contributed substantial material to the text and appendices. Among these are Dr. Ira Saltz, Associate Professor of Economics, Valdosta State University, who wrote the chapter on the Potential Costs of Technology Transfer; Dr. Niren M. Vyas, Acting Dean and Associate Professor of Marketing, School of Business Administration, University of South Carolina at Aiken, who wrote the chapter on Major Players in Technology Transfer; and Dr. Jackie Eastman, Assistant Professor of Marketing and Director of MBA Program at Valdosta State University, for her substantial contribution to the chapter on Ethical Dimensions. Dr. Jim Muncy, Associate Professor of Marketing, contributed to the chapter on Barriers and Solutions. I am also grateful to Miss Aparna Reddy, MBA, for editorial revisions of the manuscript, and to Dr. Francis W. Coleman, M.D., Valdosta, for providing excellent health care.

A Macro Perspective
on Technology Transfer

Chapter One

Introduction

This introductory chapter deals with the subject of technology transfer to less developed countries (LDCs) and related topics. First, definitions of technology and technology transfer are presented. Second, aspects such as why transfers are important, how they should be done, who the players are, the negative aspects of transfers, and what role marketing plays are discussed.

Recently, the rate of technological innovation and development has been considered a major external factor in deciding economic growth (Alkhafaji 1995; Reddy and Rao 1986). In spite of considerable economic progress made by many Third World countries during the past quarter century, it is a fact that they still have a long way to go to catch up with the developed countries (Amsalem 1983). All the evidence clearly shows that the economic gap between the developed and developing worlds would continue unabated. Development experts strongly contend that narrowing of the so-called North-South economic gap requires massive transfer of technology from the developed world to the developing world.

Despite years of help received from the developed countries, the Third World countries in Africa, Asia, and Latin America are still impoverished because of the failure of transfers. According to Arnold Pacey, programs designed to encourage transfers of technology from industrial nations to LDCs have often failed because the transfer is "imposed." Such imposed or forced technology works for a while, but eventually fails. For example, attempts to introduce tractors, water pumps, and sewage works into many African, Asian, and South American countries have failed because of the lack of customizing of machinery or processes to suit the host country's situations and needs. One way to solve this problem is to be more flexible and set up new technologies within the host country's socioeconomic framework (Pacey 1990, p. viii).

Cunningham and Sarayrah (1994) take a different view. According to them, one possible explanation for the failure of technology to transfer effectively is the human dimension—the threat of that technology to the receiving organization's internal status structure. They suggest the following solution: Seek alternative problem definitions; allow decision-making latitude at the most problematic point, using appropriate technology; and restructure the system before introducing the technology.

Marton and Singh (1991) believe that technology flows to most developing countries, measured in terms of fees and royalties for know-how and services, have continued to be very low and have tended to stagnate in most of these countries. This has been accentuated by regulatory policies and procedures that have further inhibited inflow of industrial technology to those countries that most need it. Developing countries should have a well-defined framework of policies and strategies for promotion of technology inflow and new technologies. The countries need to expand the necessary technological infrastructure, particularly human resources, and to create a suitable environment in which adequate flows of investments and new technologies can occur. These countries also need to adjust to the rapid technological changes in various production and service sectors and to develop appropriate niches in areas where new technologies can be acquired and adapted to local conditions.

There may be some hope. The problem is expected to become less severe as a techno-class of bureaucrats, engineers, and entrepreneurs in countries from Mexico to India get the necessary technology and skills. This should also make them more competitive in the second tier of technologically sophisticated economies. According to one expert, the way to gain this sophistication quickly is to leapfrog into the upper echelon of the respective technology. Everything does not have to be done from scratch. So far, India, for example, has developed customized telecommunication switches and supercomputers using parts from the West, and other Third World countries are looking to make a similar jump into modernity. Rather than wealth, the key requirements for this jump are a receptive economy and an educated and motivated population (Coy et al. 1994).

DEFINITIONS

The modern concept of a nation's growth means its technological advancements and the contributions they offer to the country's economy. Technological advancements and economic growth are the basis for classifying the world into the developed, the developing, and the undeveloped nations (Soundararajan 1983).

The term "technology" is derived from the Greek word *techne* meaning an art or skill. Technology is directed toward the use of knowledge. It is a method for doing something better. In that it requires three elements: information about the method, the means for carrying it out, and some understanding of it. The integration of these components yields a product that can be economically and socially beneficial to the development of a country.

The term "technology" is used broadly here and our discussion is limited to nonstrategic and harmless technology rather than the military or strategic high technology that is usually barred by the governments of donor nations. We will call this "low-medium technology" as opposed to the popularly known "high technology." In a broad international sense, "technology transfer" can be defined as the transfer of manufacturing and marketing technical knowledge from one country to another. Multinational firms are the major agents of transfer of technology. They transfer technologies to their subsidiaries in other countries when it fits their corporate objectives. Also, any donor firm in a developed country can transfer its technology to a recipient firm in another. The donor usually receives royalties, dividends, lump-sum payments, or some form of countertrade or barter from the recipient in return. The donor firm can also get rights to additional inventions based on the transferred technology, a feature known as "reverse engineering." Technology and technology transfer may have many meanings, depending on the orientation of the experts. We use technology transfer here in the strictest sense of its nonhazardous category. These types of low- and intermediate-level technologies are transferred to Third World nations for their economic development and general well-being. Countries strive for modern technology because technology is viewed as a tool for economic development, and to achieve higher standards of living. However, only a few countries could invest vast sums of money into research and development to reap the fruits of their endeavors today. Thus, countries like the United States, Japan, and European countries are considered as the "haves" and the rest of the world as the "have nots" of technology. Naturally, the "haves" try to protect their inventions through patenting and copyright laws. These laws are difficult to carry out globally. Policing the piracy is another safeguarding method. Such attempts to safeguard technology are not always effective. Therefore, some technology is obtained by other nations through piracy and/or copying.

Third World

The terms "Third World" or "less developed countries" (LDCs), developing countries, and developing economies mean the same in this book. Third World countries are generally those that have less than $1,000 per capita income. However, a nation could be rich because of its resources (like oil, minerals, etc.) and still be technologically far behind the developed nations. More than three-fourths of the countries in the world today fall into this category, and these countries are also generally economically and technologically underdeveloped.

On the other hand, developed countries (DCs) like the United States, Canada, Japan, Western Europe, and Australia are called the "First World." Countries in the former Soviet Union and communist countries are categorized as the "Second World." Sometimes, the oil-rich but economically underdeveloped countries are called the "Fourth World."

There is a tremendous and growing demand for basic technology from developing nations to modernize their economies and to speed up their economic development (Baranson 1969). Developed countries, including Japan, have been helping these less developed nations in this regard. However, there is much to be desired in terms of smooth and continuous flow of proper technology from developed to developing countries and to bridge the "North-South gap" between the two groups.

Traditionally, American firms have not been enthusiastic toward transfer of technology, especially to less developed nations. This is because most American firms are preoccupied with their own big, domestic market and therefore they have neglected foreign markets. Except for a few major multinational firms, such as Coca-Cola, IBM, and General Electric Corporation, most American firms have been either indifferent or lukewarm to foreign marketing. The European and Japanese firms, on the other hand, because of their historic reliance on foreign trade and their export orientation, have been more aggressive in transfer of technology to developing nations. These firms are willing to "go the extra mile" that is necessary to cultivate clients for their technology in developing nations and to nourish joint ventures once they are established.

Major Players

Major players in technology transfer are the rich developed countries. The United States, Canada, Western Europe, and Japan have the types of technologies that other countries can use. However, unless there is a benefit for them in doing so, the major players are not willing to share their technologies with other countries. Most of the transfers are made by multinational corporations (MNCs) housed in the developed countries. These MNCs transfer technologies from one branch to another to suit their corporate objectives.

THE IMPORTANCE OF THE TRANSFER

Technology transfer was not considered an important issue for development until the early 1970s (Alkhafaji 1995). With the rapid progress of technology today, it is becoming the key for economic development but also the key to sustaining the economic strength of a nation. Therefore, it is becoming difficult to persuade potential donors of technology to share their know-how with other countries. They will not share technology unless there is a justifiable benefit for them in doing so. Thus, technology transfers from developed to developing countries get more selective and limited. Typically, technologies that are relatively old or obsolete in the donor nations are transferred to other nations. Evidence of increasing importance given to issues related to technology transfer is also seen by the growth of academic and trade journals on the subject today. Additional evidence of increasing importance is the formation of organizations such as the International Executive Service Corps (IESC), founded in 1964. The IESC is committed to technology transfer through the world by helping developing countries to overcome specific problems that demand special skills, both at the conceptual and technical levels.

A well-planned technology transfer can enhance economic development in LDCs (Reddy and Rao, 1985). This will also provide future markets for the developed countries; diversification for both donor and recipient nations; benefits of reverse technology; and it could promote world order and peace because, it is hoped, people will be busier constructing their economies than going to war with others. Technology can offer hope of development to many countries that are poor and hopeless about a good future.

Economic Development

Technology can speed up the process of economic development (Reddy and Campbell 1994) and it is generally believed that technology can speed up the economic development process of the poor, less developed Third World countries. Although some Third World countries have made modest economic progress in the last few decades, most still require massive doses of appropriate technologies to keep them economically buoyant and to maintain their meager standards of living. Technology could be the way to pull them out of the vicious circle of poverty.

By developing the right infrastructure and applying modern business technology, the impoverished LDCs can build up their economic strength. However, it is the responsibility of the "haves" or the First World or the developed nations to figure out what kind of technology is needed for which country and then aggressively take necessary initiatives to offer such technologies through suitable channels.

Future Markets

Though economically poor, the LDCs hold three-fourths of the world's population. As their economic well-being is improved, they seek better products to further improve their standards of living. Developed countries could thus use these vast markets of the LDCs to sell several new products and services created for Third World countries. Recent expansion of American and European franchises in developing countries is a good example. McDonald's, Baskin Robbins, Kentucky Fried Chicken, to mention a few, are now proliferating in the markets of less developed countries.

Another rationale for technology transfer is that, as markets get saturated at home and in other developed countries, the DCs need new markets for their products—high-tech products like computers or low-tech products like electric motors, and so on. A well-developed Third World country can provide such markets. Because of the increase in incomes due to industrial growth resulting from technology transfers, these countries can afford to buy more new products and services, and will likely prefer to purchase them from those countries that help them to reach their economic development goals. Therefore, the developed countries cannot afford to ignore the vast market potential of the LDCs.

Economic Diversification

Getting into new areas of business is a great deal easier with borrowed technology than reinventing a technology that is already available somewhere else in the world. Why create technology when you can borrow it? The donor nations receive additional dividends that they may not have had otherwise. The recipient nations can diversify into many more industries that they would not otherwise have had.

Reverse Engineering

To the donor, receiving engineering or technology back from the recipient is quite beneficial. It saves time and additional research costs. Also, sometimes, it may be the only way to get to further advancements. For example, in the pharmaceutical industry, U.S. firms must abide by the many rules and regulations of the Food and Drug Administration (FDA) and other governmental agencies before introducing a new drug into the market. A foreign subsidiary of an American firm can test a drug without much hassle in its country markets and then share the information with the parent firm. With that information and background, the U.S. firm would have fewer problems in getting a drug approved by U.S. authorities for making and marketing it in the U.S. market. For example, some cancer and AIDS drugs found their way to the United States using this approach, and as by-products of reverse technology.

Psychological Well-Being, World Order, and Peace

Perhaps this may sound too ambitious, but it can be expected that when every country of the world community is busily engaged in developing its economic infrastructure through modern technology, few countries will have time to do acts that disrupt the world order and peace. Transferring appropriate technology can keep the developing countries busy building their infrastructures and welfare projects rather than fighting among themselves or with neighboring countries. They will be preoccupied with peacetime projects of building roads, hospitals, and educational facilities. Technology transfer thus can become a strategic tool for maintaining peace.

CLASSIFICATION OF TECHNOLOGIES

Technologies can be classified into various categories. They can be production or consumption type and they can be in the following categories: education, health care, manufacturing, management, marketing, sports, agriculture, engineering, space, genetics, infrastructure, telecommunication, and so on.

Basic manufacturing technology is what is immediately needed by most developing nations. These nations traditionally have been suffering from poverty caused by lack of industrial and infrastructural development and they have to import even basic manufactured goods such as bicycles and other sundry items.

Many of these nations, because of their scarce foreign exchange resources, continuously keep searching for alternatives to goods that are currently being imported. Thus, manufacturing for import substitution becomes a high priority item because it saves hard currency that can be used for other developmental needs. For example, in Nigeria, manufacturing bicycles may be more important than making automobiles. Transferring bicycle-making technology to Nigeria should not have much of a negative impact on the donor's own sales prospects in American, West European, or Japanese markets because Nigeria may not import many bicycles if it has to spend its limited hard currency to do so. Thus, by transferring bicycle-manufacturing technology, a donor firm is not only making profits but also creating some goodwill for its country. It creates new employment in the country to which the technology is transferred. This creation of goodwill can alone be an important benefit in a highly volatile modern world. Philosophically, would it not be a better way of bridging the gap between developed and developing nations? Instead of helping the less developed countries with food and clothing each time they have an emergency, it is better to show these countries how they can produce food and clothing and other necessary items for living in their own country. This can be a way of winning friends among developing nations.

According to Alkhafaji (1995), technology can be classified into four general groupings and four specific groupings. These are: process technology, product technology, application technology, and management technology.

The first of the more specific classifications includes hard and soft technology. Hard technology refers to the capital goods, blueprints, technical specifications, knowledge, and support necessary to use the technology listed above. Soft technology refers to management, marketing, finance, and administration.

The second specific classification of technology is proprietary and nonproprietary. As the name implies, proprietary technology is owned by a certain group or organization. Nonproprietary technology can be freely reproduced without infringing on proprietary rights.

The third specific classification of technology is front-end and obsolete technology. Obsolete technology is outmoded, while front-end technology is state-of-the-art.

The fourth specific grouping is bundled and unbundled technology. Bundled technology is controlled, in that the owner transfers it only as part of a package. Unbundled technology can be accessed independently.

THE TRANSFER PROCESS

There are many ways the transfer can take place. In very general terms, the first issue in the transfer is the material transfer, where new material or a new product is exported from one country to another. The second phase, design transfer, represents the ability of a firm to manufacture the new material or product in the user country. The last phase, capacity transfer, is reached when the capacity to adapt the new item to local conditions is transferred. The nature of the technology transferred, the characteristics, capabilities, and objectives of the parties involved, and the absorptive capability of specific economic and social sectors within the recipient country all affect the time required, the expense necessary, and the effectiveness of technology transfers. For example, the transfer of technology from a U.S. firm to a developing country may be slow, ineffective, and expensive, whereas a similar transfer to a developed nation may be rapid, effective, and relatively inexpensive.

INTERNATIONAL PRODUCT LIFE CYCLE THEORY

According to the international product life cycle theory, products that were once produced in developed countries are now produced in LDCs because of cost advantages in manufacturing there. Thus, once manufacturing television sets was a major industry in the United States, but now most of the television sets are manufactured in the newly industrialized countries (NICs) of Taiwan, Hong Kong, Singapore, and South Korea, or rapidly industrializing countries (RICs) such as Malaysia. In the beginning, the international product life cycle theory was a by-product of natural evolution and deliberate manipulation of multinational corporations (MNCs). Now, most of the transfers are under the control of the MNCs and very little natural evolution takes place. In other words, what technology is to be transferred when and to whom is closely monitored and regulated by concerned agencies. Some MNCs, because of public criticism of shifting employment bases to other countries, are gradually relocating manufacturing facilities to their home countries.

METHODS OF TRANSFER

The following sections briefly describe six popular approaches to technology transfer:

1. outright sale of technology;
2. equity participation or joint venture;
3. licensing;
4. direct investment with 100 percent ownership;
5. management contracts; and
6. strategic alliances.

Outright Sale of Technology

An outright sale can be defined as transfer of technology regarding a production process for a given value with no further strings attached. This is generally possible when a firm finds no further use for particular technology in its market or has no plans to use it otherwise in the future. The firm here is capitalizing on the opportunity to earn money on a technology for which it has no further use or which it cannot put to use in the markets of developing countries because of entry restrictions.

Consider, for example, the transfer of bicycle-manufacturing technology by an American firm to a firm in a developing country such as Nigeria. The American firm receives a certain negotiated fee and transfers the necessary technology. Here, the relations between the two firms end on a friendly note. However, should the Nigerian firm require additional help at a later period (if such assistance is not detrimental to the interest of the American firm), a new proposal may then be negotiated for another fee. Thus, an outright sale has advantages to both sides. The American firm will not have to supervise the operations nor periodically scrutinize the accounts of the Nigerian firm to ensure proper returns. Also, the American enterprise need not worry that the Nigerian firm may require further assistance once the deal is completed.

Equity Participation or Joint Venture

In certain countries, equity participation or joint venture may be the only way to enter their markets. In this case, an American firm may have to invest money besides transferring technology and by becoming a partner in the recipient firm. Most developing countries fix equity participation shares at a 49:51 ratio instead of 50:50 ownership; sometimes there may even be a ceiling of 25:75. In all these instances, the developing country may want to retain the controlling rights by having an edge in the ownership rights over the foreign donor firm. A common practice is for the participating donor firm to convert the fee for technology into equity shares without investing any real money. However, equity participation may be disadvantageous to the donor firm when repatriation of dividends or profits is either banned or restricted. In the latter case "how much" and "how often" one can repatriate profits can be an important consideration in the negotiation process. Since most developing countries are short of hard currency (U.S. dollars), invariably there may be some restrictions on repatriation of profits and the frequency of transfer of funds.

Another inhibiting factor for joint venture is the management methods employed by the firm in the recipient nation. More often, the donor firm might become vexed with the general management methods practiced by the recipient firm and gradually divest its interests in that firm in frustration.

Licensing

Licensing is giving away the rights to manufacture and market a firm's product(s) to a firm in a developing nation for a certain period and subject to renewals. There would be mutually negotiated initial fees and royalties that are usually calculated in terms of a percentage of annual sales. The royalty rates generally range from 5 to 10 percent of gross or net sales, depending on the bargaining strength of the parties involved and how the technology in question is viewed by the recipient country. For instance, a technology that is considered critical to a country's economic development will obtain a premium price.

Although licensing is a popular method in the pharmaceutical industry, it does not generate substantial revenues for the donor firm. But, the donor firm is not investing any money, only sharing its production technology and marketing knowledge. However, the licensor needs to supervise the operations and accounts of the licensee firm periodically to ensure production quality and use of proper market methods. Even this can be eliminated by receiving fixed amounts instead of royalties or by settling for a lump-sum fee for an agreed period.

Direct Investment with 100 Percent Ownership

Some companies, such as IBM, have a strong preference for direct investment with 100 percent ownership as a basic strategy for overseas entry and expansion. These companies transfer technologies that are very significant for socioeconomic development of the developing countries. However, these companies are often rigid about their 100 percent ownership policies in their overseas operations. Whenever the corporate policies conflict with national policies of developing countries, these corporations withdraw their operations from those countries. This is evidenced by IBM's withdrawal from India and Nigeria.

Management Contracts

Management contracting has become a major mode of technology transfer. This is especially prevalent in service industries such as hospitals, airlines, hotel management, and other service management fields. This mode of technology transfer typically results in less conflict between corporations in developed countries and the developing countries to which high technology is being transferred. This is because such management contracts typically carry provisions for the development of independent competencies within a specified time.

Strategic Alliances

Strategic alliance is similar to joint venture between two countries. However, strategic alliance, such as GM and Toyota making and selling Geo brand cars in the United States, signifies that this alliance is made to take specific marketing advantage by combining the manufacturing know-how of the Japanese Toyota Company with GM of the United States. Thus, strategic alliances are getting more popular and becoming important modes of technology transfer.

Other Forms of Transfer

International Franchising. International franchising of McDonald's, Burger King, and so on is providing yet another mode for technology transfer. Franchises offer food processing technology to carpet cleaning, service quality, product quality, record keeping, and other technologies throughout the world.

Leasing Arrangement. International leasing of heavy equipment also brings Western expertise in marketing to other countries.

Turnkey Project. Everything from manufacturing to marketing is set up in the host country, and the donor country firm hands over the project to the management of the host country and walks away. There may be a period of time (1–5 years) when engineers and consultants from the donor nations help the new management to establish itself. After that, the business is left pretty much on its own.

Other forms of dissemination of technology include publishing books and papers; holding technology seminars, symposiums, conferences, and research result presentations; acting as consultants; transfer of personnel; and holding specialized technology training courses. Due to popularity and availability of World Wide Web and Internet information systems through computers, some technologies are freely available to those who care to download software, programs, and publicly available information.

NEGATIVE ASPECTS

There is also a downside to technology transfer. First, engineers in other countries learn about new technologies in the developed countries through scientific publications, then translate them into patents and commercial products and sell them back to the countries that invented the technology in the first place. Sometimes this occurs in foreign-owned R&D sites in the United States, causing billions of dollars of lost revenue for the companies that originated the technology.

Second, the technology transfer agreements are sometimes unilateral. For example, many exchange agreements with Japan in the past have been unilateral in its favor. The United States did not get the benefit of reverse technology.

Third, many critics of technology transfer feel that it decreases a country's competitive advantage in the global market by giving away technology to an economic competitor, such as often happens with the United States and Japan, not to mention the security considerations.

In any event, conscientious and deliberate planning of technology transfer is important for both the developed and developing countries. Advance teams should be sent to developing countries to evaluate them individually and also as a group to decide whether giving away a particular kind of technology (bicycle manufacturing, for example) is universally beneficial or not.

AVOIDING RISKS

If the inherent problems and risks during technology transfer are to be avoided, there is need for both providers and receivers to make some adjustments in their respective policies and attitudes. These adjustments will greatly help the technology transfer and by that significantly contribute to narrow the North-South economic gap.

First, the providers of technology, which are the developed countries and their corporations, should adjust their policies and attitudes:

1. Technology transfer to developing countries is not only a business proposition but is an effective form of developing goodwill and enhancing international understanding.

2. The ability of the developing countries to absorb and use the technology is likely to be limited. Under these circumstances, technology transfer may not prove to be a lucrative business proposition. However, the long-term prospects and beneficial secondary effects may make such transfer highly desirable. Therefore, a long-term perspective will be required in evaluating the technology transfer proposals to developing countries.

3. The corporations in the developed countries should be prepared for a long and complicated process of negotiating the technology transfer agreements with the developing countries. The recent experiences with the Chinese bears out this problem. The companies that have patience and perseverance seem to win out in developing countries.

4. The providers of technology should endorse and accept the codes of conduct developed by the United Nations and its constituent organizations such as the UNCTAD (U.N. Conference on Trade and Development); UNIDO (U.N. Industrial Development Organization); and WIPO (World Intellectual Property Organization) (Thompson 1982).

On the other hand, developing countries should make the following adjustments in their policies and attitudes to help increase the flow of technology transfer.

1. They should recognize the beneficial effects of technology transfer on their socioeconomic development process. In the last decade this is clearly seen by the fast-paced socioeconomic development of ASEAN countries (Singapore, Malaysia, Taiwan, South Korea, and Hong Kong) and other newly industrialized countries (NICs).

2. In view of such beneficial effects, the developing countries should create more conducive conditions for the flow of technology. Besides creating the necessary infrastructure, these countries should reduce, if not eliminate, the bureaucratic delays that often prove to be major hurdles to technology transfer.

3. Instead of indiscriminately importing inappropriate technologies to their cir-

cumstances, each developing country should formulate its own policies based on realistic cost-benefit analysis of technologies desired.

4. Finally, the developing countries should accept the codes of conduct being developed by the United Nations and its constituent organizations like the aforementioned UNCTAD, UNIDO, and WIPO. Accepting such a common frame of controls by both the providers and receivers of technology will reduce many of the problems discussed previously.

TECHNOLOGY PIRATING

Stealing technology without paying for it is technology pirating. In a complex modern world, some technology pirating can happen. But firms keep track of and place barriers to the stealing of their technology. East European and Russian firms were known to steal technology when possible. Stealing is possible in the areas where buying technology is extremely expensive and in sensitive technologies that donor firms do not want to share with others.

MARKETING'S ROLE

Marketing strategy is identifying the target market and trying to reach it through marketing mix strategies, that is, product, place, price, and promotion strategies. Marketing can thus first identify the sponsors and recipients and then match the needs of the recipient firms with the availability and willingness of the donor firms' technologies. Both macro and micro marketing approaches are possible. In a macro marketing situation, the government of a country can get involved in matching the needs and transferable technologies. In a micro marketing situation, an individual firm has to make that decision, but, within the framework of its government's external policies and strategies. When Toshiba's subsidiary sold technology that improved the performance of the Russian missile launching, the U.S. government got quite upset about it.

ETHICAL DIMENSION

Technology transfer can affect the environment, economy, and culture of both the transferring and the receiving nations. It opens too many ethical dilemmas. The major problem here is the interpretation of ethics in a global situation. What is ethical to Americans may not be ethical to others and vice versa. The real problem evolves when the standards of the donor and recipient countries are at the opposites on ethical issues. In those situations, judgments must be made regarding whose ethics will dominate. Though it is difficult to decide what is right or wrong practice, serious thought must be given to ethical concerns before, during, and after technology transfer. "Human rights issues" is a major ethical concern for the developing countries in considering technology transfer.

THE PHILOSOPHY OF TECHNOLOGY TRANSFER

The philosophy of technology transfer has been that the developed countries have always been apprehensive about sharing the technologies with Third World countries for the fear of possible abuse of technology by these countries (Greenberger 1992). The Third World countries could use technologies to make and use destructive weapons, threatening world peace and order. So, most technology transfers to the Third World (except the Pacific Rim countries) are rather limited and thus do not help these countries to achieve economic growth. Chapter 3 will discuss the barriers and solutions for technology transfer to Third World countries. It has implications to policy makers on technology transfer, scholars, and the public.

CONCLUSION

This chapter introduced several important issues related to technology transfer to developing countries including the definition of some important terms used in the book. To make the transfer of technology beneficial to both donor and host nations, both parties must be realistic in their expectations of each other's perceived roles. Donors must be willing to undertake product changes, the services mix, and scale down the size of production facilities to fit the recipient nation's needs. Also, donors must not be too concerned with immediate, short-term returns; they must understand the problems in pricing and lengthy negotiation periods; recognize multiple influences, bureaucratic and communication delays; and avoid excessive concern with political uncertainties. They should also exercise patience, be empathic, and, most of all, be positive in their attitudes toward the process of transfer.

Recipient firms in developing nations must do their homework too. They should also be realistic in their expectations and demands, and prevent unwarranted delays, because inexplicable delays can only worsen the donor's perception of risks in doing business with firms in developing countries. Unfortunately, though the seemingly insurmountable problems during the gestation period may vanish over time, many projects are either abandoned, delayed, or discarded because of the impatience of the donor firms. It should be recognized that new technologies will also bring new employment, income, and standards of living into developing countries. Firms in the developed world are not only gaining profits, but also creating new and larger markets for their products and services in the future. Inasmuch as the transfer of technology will be in the control of the donor nations, the recipient nations too must develop their own resources to invent appropriate technologies needed by their unique situations. It can only be expected that the transfer process will become even more difficult in the future as it is difficult to persuade the donor nations to part with technologies that might be used by other nations to the competitive disadvantage of the donor nations.

What is most important, as the model for Technology Transfer Assimilation suggests, is that the transferred technologies be properly assimilated into the socioeconomic fabric of the country they are transferred to. Unassimilated technologies are costly and wasteful. Examples of well-assimilated technologies are automobile manufacturing, manufacturing of chemicals, and so on. Unassimilated technologies refer to technologies that include the manufacturing and marketing of products and services that are not yet needed in LDCs. There is no agency at this juncture to check on the assimilation process. But being aware of the hurdles in the assimilation should help both the donor and recipient nation to plan the transfer properly.

Chapter Two

Major Players in Technology Transfer

This chapter describes the roles of different institutions in the technology transfer process within the United States. This discussion has implications for international technology transfer in that the reader will acknowledge how technology development at the source is a complex process in itself. It is a process where governments, educational institutions, and business firms play a crucial role.

MAJOR PLAYERS

Three major institutions are involved in the transfer process:

1. Government (federal, state, local);
2. Educational institutions (universities);
3. Industry (multinational corporations, private research institutions, entrepreneurs, and inventors).

Major players are defined by their actions. For example, those that provide and act as major resources for new technologies and ideas or contribute directly to the transfer process are viewed as the major players. There are also other players acting as the facilitators. These are the venture capital firms, technology brokers, patent lawyers, and various consulting firms that identify potential licensees and clients for new technologies.

TECHNOLOGY CREATION

Governments often become heavily involved during creation and transfer of technologies. It is done at the federal, state, and local government levels. In this aspect, the U.S. government has maintained a crucial role of leadership. It establishes various governmental agencies to deal with the development and transfer of technology. It also provides funding for scientific research projects through universities and other educational institutions. This is one reason why more Nobel Prizes are won by American scientists than by any others in the world.

However, the United States does rather poorly when it comes to translating new discoveries into commercially successful products or processes. For example, at the outset, U.S. industry did not find any commercial use for the transistor, a discovery of the Bell Laboratories, New Jersey. The transistor was then sold to Japanese businesses that in turn brought out a series of different electronic products—transistor radios and television sets. These products succeeded beyond anyone's expectations in the world markets. Today, Japan holds a dominant position in the electronics market and has for the last three decades, making it a very rich country.

Similarly, the technology of the recording head of the VCR was also purchased by the Japanese from U.S. research laboratories. Now the Japanese hold the patent on VCR recording heads. More than 90 percent of the VCRs sold throughout the world have Japanese recording heads. It is a position that the Japanese have been enjoying for the last two decades. Think of the enormous profits the Japanese businesses make on this product alone!

Perhaps the main reason for the inability of the United States to capitalize on its invention is the difficulty of coordinating the transfer process. Within the United States, there are some difficulties in harnessing innovation into commercially successful products. It takes a tremendous amount of coordination and cooperation among the three key players, particularly when each player may have goals that do not coincide with those of the others.

The technology transfer model suggested by Amidon Rogers (1989) is shown in Figure 2.1. The model suggests that interaction among key players enhances creativity that ultimately should result in innovation. However, for the transfer process to be profitable, the invention should be taken all the way to the commercialization stage. Bruce Merryfield (1983) suggests that for the technology transfer process to be successful, creativity and knowledge must move through three stages consecutively:

Figure 2.1
Total R&D Worldwide

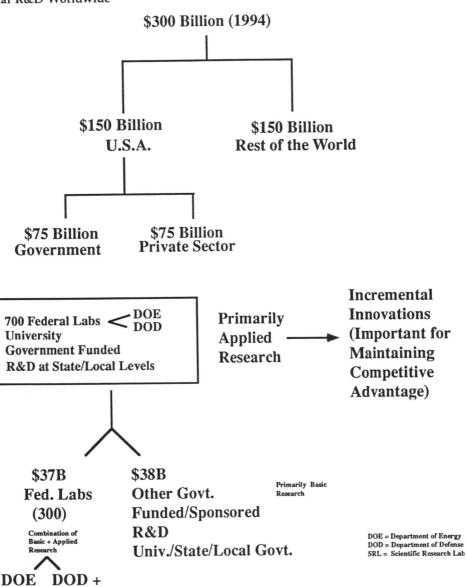

1. Invention
2. Translation
3. Commercialization

It is observed that the role of universities and government is direct and active in the first stage. It changes to collaborative and supportive in the second stage, and almost nonexistent in the final stage.

The opposite is the case with respect to the role of the industry or the private sector. Participation and the commitment by the private sector increase as the process moves through the first two stages. They virtually take over the process during the final stage of commercialization.

THE ROLE OF GOVERNMENTS

What role do governments play in the technology transfer process? How do they play this role? Some governments invest heavily in the development of science and technology for reasons such as defense, infrastructure, and intellectual development. Thus, for many reasons, most governments take an active role regarding development and transfer of the technology. The U.S. government has always played a dominant role in this respect.

The United States

The data shown in Figure 2.1 indicate that total R&D expenditure worldwide in 1994 was about $300 billion (*Business Week* 1994, p. 75). Half of that, about $150 billion, was spent in the United States. Again, half of the $150 billion ($75 billion) is spent by the U.S. government in various federal research labs. In other words, the U.S. government spends almost 25 percent of world R&D dollars and thus represents a major source for technical knowledge and innovations. Until 1980, the availability of inventions made in the government labs was extremely limited to the private sector industry or universities. Working under contract with federal labs, small businesses and nonprofit companies had difficulties in getting the title to inventions conceived during their own work. However, policy makers recognized that they could not ignore the output of one-sixth of the technological work force. This consists of the collective output of more than 100,000 engineers and scientists in more than 700 labs. The Bay-Dole Act of 1980, however, attempted to correct that problem. Also, the Stevenson-Wyler Act of 1980 has allowed federal labs to share the technologies developed with U.S. industry. However, when these two actions did not produce anticipated results, much stronger legislation, the Technology Transfer Act of 1986, was passed. It placed the Department of Energy (DOE) labs under the technology transfer umbrella and required all federal labs to establish a technology transfer office as liaison with the industry. It also encouraged nonfederal institutes to participate. Furthermore, it favored licensing of inventions and sharing of royalties with the inventors.

With U.S. manufacturing on the decline, and still little actual technology emerging from federal labs, an aggressively written National Competitiveness Technology Transfer Act was passed in 1989. It required labs to establish objectives and milestones for carrying out R&D. It also focused on cooperative R&D between industry and academic institutions. The challenge for the 1990s is for U.S. industry and the federal R&D facilities to work together closely to realize the promise of the legislation of 1980. Since this legislation was passed, several methods have evolved for taking technology out of the labs, with each lab adopting the methods that best fit its particular policies, contract requirements, and industry needs.

METHODS OF TRANSFER

Licensing

The most common method is licensing intellectual property. Inventions, for example, may be patented, and the patents are then available for licensing from the federal agency or the lab's contracted operator. A natural outgrowth of licensing is the need for a lab to provide consulting help to an industrial licensee or to exchange personnel with it. Such consulting agreements are carefully examined to avoid conflicts of interest, and licensees pay fees to ensure that the government is adequately compensated. Such personnel exchanges can also benefit the lab and the industrial partner.

Joint Research

Because most lab-developed technology is very preliminary, a great amount of development is required to take that technology from initial licensing to commercial success. Joint research between industry and lab can effectively carry out that development. Cooperative Research and Development Agreements (CRADAs) formalize this cooperative effort. Model CRADAs containing standard terms and conditions are maintained by various government agencies running R&D facilities. If the model CRADA is acceptable to the individual partner, it can be carried out quickly. Important provisions of CRADAs include:

- The lab is not allowed to contribute funds to the project but is expected to provide personnel and facilities. The industrial partner, however, may provide funds to the lab.
- Information developed under the CRADA that is proprietary can be protected from access under the Freedom of Information Act for a period not exceeding five years. Proprietary information contributed by the industrial partner and properly identified is not subject to disclosure.
- Each party to the CRADA is responsible for complying with export control regulations.
- Parties to the agreement have the first option to title inventions created by their employees. The government agency, however, retains a nonexclusive, non-transferable, irrevocable, paid-up license to practice or have practiced for the United States every invention created under CRADAs.

Contract Research

A more traditional method of working with federal labs is contract research, called "work for other," which cannot compete with for-profit businesses. The industrial partner is charged full cost for the lab work, an amount that could exceed private sector costs. However, the industrial partner gains access to facilities and knowledge that cannot be duplicated without government's help. Inventions that spring from this relationship are automatically titled to the industrial partner in advance through class patent waivers.

The Department of Energy

Another opportunity for interaction with government labs is doing research at unique technological user facilities at the labs. The DOE, for example, has about 200 of these facilities. Using such facilities should accelerate development of technologies and reduce R&D costs for industry.

Gaining access to labs' technology is best done through personal contacts with technical specialists at the lab. In searching for the right technology, however, the most effective sources are the Federal Laboratory Consortium (FLC) for Technology Transfer at the national level, and the Office of Technology Transfer at the laboratory level.

Instituted to make more effective use of federally developed technology and inventions, the FLC is a service organization made up of technology transfer representatives from each lab. It helps industrial companies in identifying the labs best suited to address their technological needs.

More than 300 of the largest federal R&D labs representing twelve federal agencies are members of the FLC. They are the departments of

Agriculture, Commerce, Defense, Energy, Health and Human Services, Interior, Justice, and Transportation, and the EPA, NASA, the National Science Foundation, and the Tennessee Valley Authority.

The FLC holds two national meetings annually, as well as general sessions, special sessions, and workshops to discuss new policies, directions, and methods relevant to technology transfer.

Larger laboratories have an office of technology transfer with staff knowledgeable in that lab's capabilities and technologies. These offices, which also frequently house the lab's intellectual property, can be contacted through the lab's controlling agency.

With the end of the Soviet Union, the federal labs have lost their traditional focus on developing weapons and defenses aimed at countering the Soviet threat. The United States is unwilling to dismantle the technological powerhouse those labs represent. The government is making every effort to refocus the lab's activities on commercial applications and to get them working more closely with private firms. The norms, values, and the culture in federal labs are changing. This is shown by the contents of the message from Admiral James D. Watkins, Secretary of Energy under the Bush administration, to the DOE employees.

One of the highest priorities in the 1990s is to promote U.S. industrial competitiveness through technology transfer. The science and technology developed in DOE research programs, laboratories, and nonlaboratory facilities helps to form a knowledge base that is one of the most valuable national assets.

One can make a major contribution to the country's economic well-being by supporting technology transfer programs that help make this knowledge base available in both the private and public sectors. The 1993 Defense Authorization Act outlined the Technology Reinvestment Project (TRP) as part of defense conversion policy. On March 11, 1993, President Clinton declared that there are two things government can do: promote dual-use research and promote the civilian use of technology that was formerly developed for military purposes. The uniqueness of technologies available from federal labs is that they have dual use, both military and commercial applications. The ultimate goal is the development of cutting-edge, military-industrial capability within healthy, commercially based companies.

Japan

Japanese officials and industry leaders are eager to foster invention in Japan. Most of the technologies on which they have built their economic successes were initially imported from the West. However, the situation has changed. Japan is catching up with the West in scientific achievement in many areas. Japan is becoming an increasing source of new technology for the rest of the world. For example, in 1990 the United States spent $490 million to license Japanese technology (Moffat 1991, pp. 84–96).

The Japanese government has set up the national research institutes to establish the R&D policies of the ministries and other public sector organizations that receive the bulk of central research funding. The major groups are supported by a division of the Ministry of International Trade and Industry (MITI). They spend the major share of basic research funds, mainly on the physical sciences, although they often carry out some health sciences research. Many programs have been initiated, such as the Creative Science and Technology Promotion system, to encourage collaborative projects. They attempt to create different organizational and group structures within selected laboratories. The idea is that from its position at the forefront of technology in several fields, Japan can no longer rely on others to supply the generic technologies. Several of these collaborative projects include non-Japanese partners (Schmid 1991).

The government has also set up many special groups to foster Western-style research programs. ERATA (Exploratory Research for Advanced Technology) was set up in 1981 to sponsor five-year research projects. They are staffed by young researchers from the private sector and universities, and sometimes include foreign scientists. While officially supporting the need to expand basic research, the Japanese government has shown reluctance to expand research funding to the levels of the United States or other Western industrial countries.

In other MITI-directed collaborative projects, there is a variation in the proportion of the research that is carried out cooperatively and that which is done separately within company labs. A delicate balance is sought between competition and cooperation. The main contribution the Japanese government has made to industrial organizations is the provision of subsidies for research. It also helped companies to devote additional attention to the technology transfer process. It implies that MITI plays an important role in spotting new areas, later perceived by the companies to be profitable and helpful in creating competitive advantage. It is placing increasing importance on the take-up of new technology by industry, especially by the participating companies.

MITI retains ownership of the patents, and companies must pay royalties for a license. Companies work separately when it comes to prototype development and commercialization, and there is no cooperation at this point.

The Japan Industrial Technology Association (JITA) has the role of making the results of national institutes' R&D available to industry and of supporting interactions between industries and research institutes. JITA does not confine its activities to Japan. It presents the latest technology developed in the institutes to overseas audiences for technology transfer. It has a total of about 20,000 patents and technologies, of which about 2,500 have been licensed. Interestingly, the Japanese government is not concerned with short-term financial measures of success. Its main focus is on long-term success in key technologies to retain an edge in the global marketplace.

Germany

The German government recognizes the need for basic research on a broad scale, including applied research and technology development. This need is carried out through basic research programs in the universities, the Max Planck Institutes, and private sector research labs (Redwood 1991; CEST 1991). Funding comes from federal, state, and private sector sources. Germany also participates in the European Community (EC) joint projects.

The Fraunhofer Institutes are well recognized for working at the interface between industry and universities and are the main location for formal contract research and development. They also offer technological information and advisory services (FHG 1988). Initially these institutes were heavily supported by the government. However, they have been so successful that they are now funded only 50 percent by the government; the remaining 50 percent comes from industry.

The institutes are on university premises and often use young university personnel. Senior engineers and scientists in the institutes have normally worked for ten to fifteen years in industry or government agencies after receiving their doctorates. When they come to work for the institutes, they have extensive experience and contacts in industry.

The German system recognizes that different mechanisms for technology transfer are needed to serve different functions in the spectrum of relationships between basic and applied research scientists, within small, medium, and large companies. It understands the importance of good communications channels and tries to achieve this by whatever is the most effective means. There is no attempt to standardize on any specific model of technology transfer process.

France

In France, the research is carried out in both higher education institutions and government institutions. The government provides substantial funding for research and development over a wide range of basic and applied research. In the recent past, the directions of technology and the transfer efforts were centralized. Recently, there has been a determined and effective drive to create a network of regional centers.

Many regions in France have very comprehensive programs for economic development. They consist of joint university and industry projects linked to the economic needs of the area. The Regional Council of Brittany in 1989 set up an agency, BRITTA, to coordinate a comprehensive array of services and financial aids to support technology transfer into local industry. Its offerings include grants to help fund joint research between institutes and companies, financial assistance to find licenses and knowledge, and many other inducements to encourage development of a local, high technology. The French government institution known as Centre National de la Recherche Scientifique (CNRS) carries out 20 percent of French public research in its 1,300 labs. Its mission is fundamental research, but it also considers the needs of the industry. Industry in this case means French enterprises, or foreign-owned companies that provide employment, preferably in R&D, in France (Duby 1985). The center also organizes clubs that bring together its own researchers with members from several companies, usually large, to look at specific technological issues. It sometimes sends researchers to industry for a couple of years for cross-training. CNRS will patent and license its own technology. It also has funds and facilities to carry out predevelopment work. It appropriates a share of royalty stream to the inventory and to the individual lab.

The Institut National de al Santé et de la Research Medicale, known as INSERM, has 250 research centers concerned with medical, biomedical, and public health research. The Agence National de la Valorisation de la Recherche (ANVAR) is the main central government organization with responsibility for technology transfer. It has twenty-two regional offices to advise and help industry. Its main objectives are to encourage industrial innovation, to evaluate the research work carried out in universities and institutes, and to help industry to access the international markets. It plays an important role as coordinator between companies and French public sector researchers. It will seek overseas licensing of French inventions and is currently very active in promoting international joint ventures (ANVAR 1989). The organization is proud of its record in helping smaller companies and claims to have aided more than 13,000 French companies.

During the last few years, the French regions have been encouraged to set up their own centers of innovation and technology transfer, known as CRITT. These are beginning to play an important role in coordinating local industry and universities, and in offering information services, consultation, and financial support. CRITT and ANVAR also advise companies and research and development projects.

France has set up a number of major programs to boost French technological competitiveness. Recently, however, there is an increasing emphasis on European collaborative programs.

United Kingdom

The first truly collaborative program involving universities, industry, and government was initiated in 1981 by the Department of Trade and Industry (DTI) in the United Kingdom. The DTI has set up a number of programs to help industry and academic collaboration. These include the Teaching Company Scheme, involving academics in a long-term constancy relationship with an individual company, and the Link Scheme, which supports research collaboration between companies and university scientists over a wide range of technological areas. The United Kingdom also participates in many major international research programs encouraging technological competitiveness. These include all the EC R&D projects and the American Strategic Defense Initiative.

In 1988 the DTI published a White Paper promising a greater emphasis on technology transfer, especially between educational institutions and industry (DTI 1989). The need to make better use of academic resources is specifically recognized; helping the diffusion of important new technologies is a major goal.

British industries and academics have become much more sophisticated partners in joint ventures. Skills in managing joint projects vary among institutions, but the general level of understanding of industrial needs and how they can be reconciled with institutional objectives is quite high. This means that interactions with universities have become a more fruitful and attractive option.

The importance of transferring technology is now recognized in British publicly funded research. Most have developed policies on exploitation and, to a variable degree, they have created the structures and facilities to carry it out.

THE ROLE OF THE PRIVATE SECTOR IN TECHNOLOGY TRANSFER

The cost of in-house research and development is escalating at a steady pace in the private sector. Simultaneously, the risk of product development is also increasing due to shortening of product life cycle. The rapid spread of scientific knowledge combined with specialization in specific technological fields has created an interesting situation. No one company can expect to dominate all technologies. Even giants like IBM have begun forging strategic alliances to obtain crucial technologies not available in-house. For example, developing a semiconductor chip is becoming so risky that IBM is teaming up with Siemens of Germany to develop 64 megabyte DRAMS for sale in the mid-1990s. The interfirm licensing and strategic alliances, together with incremental innovations, will become the backbone of new product development efforts in the future. To spread the necessary financial commitments and to reduce the risk of permanent losses by participants in the race, firms will increasingly share technologies through the technology transfer process.

Technology transfer is becoming an attractive mechanism to obtain new technologies for a firm. Growing numbers of international companies are willing to engage in collaboration over long distances. In addition, it is no longer unusual for companies to have R&D facilities near universities in other countries, to be near the source of invention. For example, many international companies including Switzerland's Ciba-Geigy and Japan's Yamanouchi now have R&D labs in the United Kingdom.

Japanese academic and industrial liaisons until recently came in two major forms: one in which both parties were Japanese, the other in which the corporate partner was Japanese and the academic partner non-Japanese. This is beginning to change (Moffat 1991). There are now instances of Western companies working with Japanese scientists. Where they occur, the companies are Japan-based subsidiaries of foreign companies. This may be more a function of Western reluctance to learn to read Japanese and to locate in Japan than of Japanese desire to exclude foreign interests (Moffat 1991). On the whole, foreigners visiting or working in Japan report a very communicative atmosphere, and greater availability of information about scientific and technological developments (Bower 1991).

Japanese industry is not investing solely in Japanese science. Companies are spending lavishly abroad on basic research projects. They have taken with enthusiasm to collaborative relationships with Western universities, and with small, R&D-based companies that maintain close academic links. The electronics giant NEC has set up a research institution in the United States at Princeton to accommodate work in areas that it hopes will ultimately help development of new products such as "interpretation telephone" that will translate automatically. Hitachi has extended its R&D network to Dublin, Cambridge (U.K.), California, and Michigan, where it has set up labs.

In Germany, many programs for technology transfer are supported mainly by industry. This is an indication that these programs have been of great benefit to the industrial sector (Redwood 1991). This is born out by the high level of importance attributed to them by senior German executives in a survey of services of technology carried out by the English Center for Exploitation of Science and Technology (CEST 1991).

In the past, France has followed strong nationalistic policies, and 25 percent of manufacturing industry is in government hands (Stoffaes 1984). This is changing, and now there is increasing emphasis in French industries on European collaborative projects that will enhance the technology transfer process.

From a communications perspective, it is a small world, and getting smaller. This has tremendously enhanced the technology transfer process globally. Large, small, and medium-size companies are continuously scanning the globe for new technologies. The companies in the private sector are constantly exchanging information among themselves through trade shows, exhibits, and other mechanisms such as licensing, strategic alliances, joint ventures, and partnerships. The interaction mechanisms also are in place among the three key players: government, industry, and academia. The role of universities and higher education in the technology transfer process is examined in the next section.

THE ROLE OF ACADEMIA IN TECHNOLOGY TRANSFER

Innovations derived through universities are increasingly recognized as a major source of new technology, both for large companies and for small new companies. The role of universities in helping to create new, technology-based companies with considerable growth potential was recognized in the 1960s. Stanford and MIT had spun out several companies, exploiting technology invented in the universities. With continuing support from the academic institutions, the new ventures grew rapidly, and in their turn spun out more companies. These continued to cluster around the supportive area of the parent institutions (Dorfman 1983; Saxenian 1983). At the same time, large companies began to set up R&D facilities near the campuses to help technology transfer. Often the large firms had long-standing, collaborative relationships with these universities. This phenomenon attracted considerable interest around the world, and the critical features of industrial liaison activities at these institutions were closely examined.

The first European attempt to duplicate Stanford and MIT in this respect was at Heriot-Watt University in Scotland. In the years since then, several British attempts have been made to build new companies or strengthen established firms with university-derived technology.

Science parks are springing up throughout the United States, Europe, and the Far East. Some have been operating for quite a long time, but the vast majority were founded after 1980. The founders of such parks are usually the universities in collaboration with local government and local financial institutions. They include the initial research facilities, incubators and offices, services, and sometimes housing. The landscaping and layout are an important part of the general attractiveness of the location. The less visible parts of the infrastructure are equally important for maintaining the growth potential of the park. This period typically takes several years, during which new companies start to set up in the park. Often these are direct or indirect spin-offs from the university. This is the period that generates new, highly skilled jobs and the beginning of the economic returns in the shape of a lively, innovative local private sector.

The Research Triangle Park of North Carolina was founded in the late 1950s to encourage high-technology industry to locate in North Carolina. The founders were a group of influential financiers, industrialists, and politicians. Private and state funds were used in its initial phase. The park is managed by a foundation that returns profits from the park to support joint research and educational projects involving the three universities linked to the park. The early tenants were major companies such as Monsanto and IBM. By 1986, 20,000 people worked in 35 organizations in the park (Waugman 1986). However, the first organization to set up in the park was a nonprofit research institute that carried out collaborative projects between university scientists and private or public sponsors. There has been more emphasis on small business development in recent years.

Sweden, Germany, and France have opened research parks near universities. Sweden's Novum Research Park, officially opened in 1990, is expected to house both Swedish and foreign companies developing health care products. It has close links with the Karolinska Institute and its medical school, which has a research institution in the park. It has planned to build a new, research-oriented international university in the park itself, around a nucleus of professors already in the Karolinska Institute Medical and Orthodontology Schools.

Medical Park in Hanover, Germany, projected to become Europe's premier bioscience center, was founded in 1987. Germany is Europe's biggest center for pharmaceutical and medical electronics companies. Hanover has more than 100 educational centers, with the medical school next door to the park.

Sophia Antipolis, in the Maritime French Alps, is a science park on a grand scale. It was set up in 1969 and now houses many companies, including multinationals, research organizations, and labs of the University of Nice.

In Japan, Tsukuba Science City was set up by moving a university out to Tokyo to a country site, surrounding it with government research institutions, and inviting large companies to set up R&D centers on the periphery. Another park is planned in Japan that contains the prestigious Kyoto University.

Business School Faculty

Presently there is a lack of awareness among business schools about the subject of the technology transfer. Few colleges or universities have courses in this area. There is some work being carried out on a consulting basis at universities, but the number of faculty involved is very small. It is not, however, a subject area that business students are exposed to in any detail. Only a limited amount of research has been conducted in this area (Vyas and Shelburn 1992). As a result, most business faculty members are not even considering this area as a part of the business school curriculum. The faculty of business schools need to be alerted to the importance of this subject to prepare the students—the future business managers—to understand the process of technology transfer.

There are several means by which technology transfer can be made an integral part of the business curriculum. A starting point is to add a course in this area to the marketing curricula. At some schools, it might be appropriate to even formulate a concentration or major in technology transfer.

The closest course to this subject area presently being offered is Industrial Marketing. However, technology transfer receives only limited coverage in this course. Even the International Marketing course barely alerts students to the need for better implementation of technology transfer process in the global arena. Many marketing students, however, do not take either of these courses, especially at the undergraduate level, and therefore miss even a limited exposure to the issue of technology transfer.

Another means by which technology transfer can be promoted is to present the idea both formally and informally at professional meetings and conferences. In this way, the faculty who are often most active in research will be reached. Also, special attention could be paid to deans who would be most influential in having a course or concentration in technology transfer adopted.

Marketing faculty could also conduct seminars in technology transfer for the business community. These seminars would encourage the interaction between academia and business that is needed to make technology transfer successful. To create awareness among students, technology transfer can be integrated into several courses in the marketing curriculum. It involves updating courses to reflect the basic understanding of the process.

A technique that offers significant advantages is an internship course in technology transfer for outstanding students at the senior level in undergraduate or graduate study, with practical experience on how to market new technology. Figure 2.1 suggests how the marketing faculty could play a leadership role in the technology transfer process (Vyas and Shelburn 1992).

The importance of the technology transfer process is recognized at the highest levels in the state of South Carolina. A special curriculum committee has been established that includes faculty members from business, law, and engineering schools from four major universities in South Carolina. The goal is to include the topic of technology transfer in each of the core courses offered at these schools. In addition, an elective course on technology transfer will be offered at both the undergraduate and graduate levels (Vyas and Moorehouse 1993).

Problems

Historically, in the United States there has been a reluctance by business to become involved with government in developing new products. Business has attempted for the most part to remain separate from government. This was not a problem in the past. However, with resurgence of other major economic powers after World War II, this strategy is no longer feasible. In Japan and in Europe, the government works much more closely with industry, often helping to finance businesses so that they can be competitive in world markets.

Another barrier to technology transfer is the perception held by the private sector about federal government. They believe that dealing with federal bureaucracy is difficult, time-consuming, and nonproductive. There is also a problem of communications among federal labs, academia, and the private sector. Each group has differing perspectives with respect to research. Business executives believe that federal labs are far removed and insulated from the business world and have little idea about how it operates. Researchers in the federal labs and academia, on the other hand, believe that U.S. businesses focus too much on short-term profits and therefore fail to carry out long-term R&D strategies.

Reluctance by U.S. companies to adopt technologies from outside is an additional barrier to technology transfer. Such behavior is known as NIH (Not Invented Here) syndrome. One study of 50 large Japanese firms and 75 large U.S. firms found that Japanese companies spend less time and money developing new products, simply because the Japanese were quick at exploiting innovations made elsewhere (Scherer 1992). At the same time, American firms were trying to generate more of their innovations internally.

The distinction between "market pull" and "technology push" are not always clear to the federal labs that act as barriers to technology transfer. The market pull is a problem looking for a solution, while technology push is a solution looking for a problem. Many inventions from federal labs were made for specific purposes or applications of defense needs. The challenge of the technology transfer process is to find where such invention could be applied successfully in the private sector, that is, to identify a problem in the private sector that the technology from federal labs will resolve. In other words, it is a solution looking for a problem. Federal labs often hand industry a "black box," explain the workings, and hope for success in the marketplace. In reality this is an extremely challenging task and ideally requires very close relationships between labs and the private sector. Such relationships remain difficult to forge (Vyas, Kauffman, and Rogers 1994).

When a license is granted to a business firm by a federal lab, it is usually nonexclusive, meaning another firm could apply and obtain a license for the same technology. Such policy is a threat to the "competitive advantage" a firm may try to create with the technology found. Many private firms are discouraged by this policy. Exclusive licensing by federal labs raises legal issues, since all taxpayers have equal rights to the invention from the lab.

Many inventions from federal labs are in their conceptual stage and require large amounts of development efforts to bring these innovations to the marketplace. These "maturation issues" are yet another barrier to technology transfer.

Solutions

1. The NIH (Not Invented Here) syndrome could be overcome by communicating the importance of technology transfer to business executives through seminars, conferences, and publications in the professional journals.
2. Federal labs have made tremendous progress in reducing bureaucracy in dealing with them. Specific examples of such progress and their willingness to interact with the private sector should be communicated to business executives.
3. The labs and academia may bring industry into the R&D pipeline earlier when necessary. Their goal is to undertake more R&D initiative with industry from the start. Through increased collaboration and cost sharing in all phases of R&D, everyone can understand the market relevance and help to move the resulting innovations into the market in parallel with continuing R&D.
4. The natural outgrowth of licensing is the need for the licensor (labs) to provide consulting help or to exchange personnel with an industrial license.
5. Individuals in the federal labs and in academia who are responsible for technology transfer must also help business entrepreneurs to evaluate risks involved in new development by providing information on these innovations. How far along is the development? How comprehensive would a license be? Are the current researchers available to carry on the effort? What are the competing technologies and the developments? What else is coming over the horizon? Answers to these questions will help the technology transfer process toward potential licensing in the private sector. Here again, business schools can help federal labs and academia researchers to conduct preliminary market feasibility studies, and provide answers to these questions that are critical for the process.

THE ROLE OF MULTINATIONAL CORPORATIONS

Unnoticed by the public, the proprietary kind of technology is transferred by multinational corporations within its local and international

operations. International Business Machines (IBM), for example, will decide what and how much technology it has to transfer to its Brazilian
subsidiary. Market, profit, and competitive considerations decide these
transfers. Since most of this is unpublished, it is difficult to estimate the
transfers.

TECHNOLOGY TRANSFER: ENCOURAGING RESULTS

Success of technology transfer efforts is difficult to measure. The bot-
tom-line goals of increased employment, tax revenues, and gross national
product (GNP) may not be directly traceable to technology transfer efforts. Some indirect measures, such as patents and licenses granted, however, are tracked.

A 1991 study by the GAO (General Accounting Office) examined
twelve federal agencies that accounted for approximately 97 percent of
the federal R&D funds. From 1980 to 1990, these agencies applied for
15,699 patents and received 11,075, a 70 percent success rate. They also
negotiated 1,436 licenses that produced $37.5 million in income over that
same period. The average number of licenses granted rose from 130 annually during 1981–1986 to 164 annually during 1987–1990 (Vyas, Corey,
and Hooker 1994).

While these agencywide increases are modest, a number of individual
federal labs are experiencing a phenomenal growth in licensing and in
the number of cooperative contracts with industry partners in R&D. At
the DOE (Department of Energy) Savannah River Site (SRS), for example,
a program started in 1989 to encourage filing inventions disclosures
yielded an increase of patent applications from a rate of about one per
year to the current rate of one per week. The number of patents issued
has also increased at a similar rate. Through the first nine months of
1993, nine licenses were negotiated, compared with only two granted
since 1989. Oak Ridge National Lab and the Ames Laboratory Center for
Advanced Technology Development are experiencing similar results.

CONCLUSION

More innovations in a wide range of technologies are taking place now
than in any previous era. An interesting characteristic of present trends
in technological development is that they are often closely intertwined
with contemporary advances in basic science. Sheer abundance of new
technologies and innovations is creating newer possibilities. This is one
of the major forces driving the key players in the technology transfer
process. The universities and the government R&D facilities are seen to
be an important source, not just of the ultimate intellectual roots of new
technologies, but of commercially viable skills and patentable inventions.

In that, business schools, along with the engineering and science schools, can contribute to helping industry to bring these inventions successfully to the marketplace. Collaboration among industry, academia, and government will always require some willingness by these institutions to be adaptable. Whenever possible, the rules of the relationships should be clarified up front. They must also be modifiable, by mutual consent, as the situation dictates, but at any one time the operating framework should be well understood by all parties. Clear objectives and regular monitoring are necessary. While this situation is typical in the United States, foreign countries may not have equal access to these innovations.

Chapter Three

Barriers and Solutions

This chapter presents a discussion related to barriers and solutions in transferring technology to developing countries. Research on the Internet showed more than one hundred references on the subject of technology transfer. Yet, very few articles address problems related to technology transfer to Third World countries.

Barriers to technology transfer are different among various industrial sectors—manufacturing, service, agribusiness, and mining. The types of technology transferred, the reasons for transferring the technology, and the channels of transfer are different in each sector, depending on company policies, preferences, and products. Industrial sectors and companies assess the host country environment differently. Furthermore, the infrastructure available to technology is different in each host country. As a result, the technological contributions made to the host country vary. The barriers to transfers and the impacts of technology transfer differ according to the outcome of negotiations between companies and government as well as between licensor and licensee. Most trade-offs are made because of these negotiations, and the trade-offs differ according to industrial sector, company policies, and government negotiating abilities. Each of these aspects of technology transfer needs to be examined separately for each of the major industrial sectors to develop sound policies (Behrman 1978, p. 17).

Technology transfer to Third World countries is quite active. For instance, AT&T recently reached a technology transfer and manufacturing deal with China. China will get new switching gear and other telecommunications technology from AT&T and AT&T in return gets access to the vast Chinese telecommunications market. Banerjee and Chakravorty

(1994, p. 71) report the successful transfer of modern city planning technology to Calcutta through help from the Ford Foundation.

THE PHILOSOPHY OF TECHNOLOGY TRANSFER

The philosophy of technology transfer has been that the developed countries have always been apprehensive about sharing the technologies with Third World countries for fear of possible abuse of technology by these countries (Greenberger 1992). The Third World countries could use technologies to make and use destructive weapons, threatening world peace and order. So, most technology transfers to the Third World (except the Pacific Rim countries) are rather limited and thus have not helped these countries to achieve economic growth. The purpose of this chapter is to discuss the barriers and solutions for technology transfer to Third World countries. It has implications for policy makers on technology transfer, scholars, and the public.

BARRIERS

Major barriers in the transfer process slow the technology transfer. The barriers encompass many issues between the donor and recipient nation. These include a variety of problems related to communication, socioeconomic and cultural differences, differences in ethical viewpoints, and so on. Sometimes the donors or recipients themselves reject offers of technology or simply are unable to use the given technology to its maximum extent. The issues here include the mismatch, need for product modification, short-run concern for quick sales and profits, false expectations on both sides, long negotiation periods, multiple influences, and fears of political uncertainty.

The Mismatch

There is often an enormous difference between what developing countries need and what developed nations are willing to offer (Goulet 1977). Quite often, developing countries are in need of manufacturing technology for products outdated in developed nations. However, many firms in developed nations are reluctant to retrieve and customize production of technology that is no longer in use. For example, a firm that currently produces sophisticated electronic typewriters may have produced standard typewriters several decades ago. Many developing nations possess an environment that is not conducive to the use of advanced technology. For instance, it could be quite difficult to convince a typist in a town where there are frequently recurring power failures to use a modern electric or electronic typewriter. In this type of environment, a standard office typewriter may be preferred over an electronic typewriter. Additionally, lack of repair and service facilities may inhibit the choice of a high-tech typewriter compared with a more conventional and basic type.

Need for Product Modifications

Often there is the need for minor changes in a product to suit the conditions of a developing country. This requires some effort from the R&D department of the donor firm, which may not be too enthusiastic about it since the department is constantly in pursuit of a better technology to outperform the competition. Therefore, to persuade the R&D staff to go through the process of "reverse engineering" could become a Herculean task for top management. For instance, one can wonder how responsive the R&D staff of RCA Corporation would be if asked to design a hand-cranked phonograph or gramophone to be marketed in villages in or near the Sahara Desert where these people have poor access to electricity or batteries. An alternative could be to design a solar-powered gramophone, which would be a high-tech product with a matching price tag so high that the poor in the Sahara could not afford to buy it.

Levels of Technology

Most developing countries do not have sophisticated infrastructures such as modern transportation methods, banking and insurance facilities, or sophisticated customers. Under these circumstances, donor firms have to adjust and adapt the level of technology to meet the needs of consumers in these countries. However, many business firms in developed countries are used to thinking in terms of improving the level of their technology rather than switching back to a lower level of technology to create, test, and market products suitable to low- or intermediate-level technological environments.

Investors' Concern Over Short-Term Profits

There is great concern for immediate volume sales by many donor firms who do not realize the marketing difficulties in developing countries. Although many developing countries are highly populated and, therefore, offer potentially large markets, these markets need to be cultivated, a process that takes a long time, even in developed countries. It may take longer in developing countries because they generally lack modern marketing methods and know-how (efficient distribution and promotion methods). The distribution systems in developing nations are usually quite different from those in modernized countries. A manufacturer either has to rely on a single wholesaler (who will demand excessive credit facilities) or directly distribute the product, which often proves to be a prohibitively expensive method of distribution.

According to the "adoption curve" concept, a new product goes through a series of steps before it is accepted by most consumers. First, a few people buy and try the product; second, these are followed by an early majority; and, finally, by a late majority, by which time 90 percent of the prospects have accepted the new product. The length of the curve (adoption time) varies by product class—luxury products take a longer time compared to necessities. The adoption curve usually takes six months to three years in advanced countries, depending on the product type. It could take longer in developing countries because of low purchasing power, illiteracy, poor communication, and lack of media availability for promotion. Even when media are available, their use may be closely regulated by the government, and may be very expensive. However, donor firms are generally reluctant to wait for longer adoption periods. Therefore, a project that has no immediate cash return prospect is either rejected or cold-shouldered, despite the realities of the situation in a given developing nation.

Unrealistic Expectations

Some donor firms expect not only quick cash returns but also substantial up-front fees even before the project is commenced. They justify these expectations with their perception that they are doing the "poor" recipient firms a favor. On the other hand, many recipient firms expect the donor firms to invest heavy capital because of their perceived huge market potential and the expectation that the rich donor firm will capitalize on it. In reality, rarely is there a match between expectations. This is one important reason for abandonment of many potentially sound projects. A solution to these premature ends of projects is for both sides to do some groundwork before they meet, to discuss the prospects for cooperation, and to be considerate in their expectations of the other's role.

Pricing Problems

Because of its strength compared to other hard currencies (the German mark, English pound, and Japanese yen), the U.S. dollar often commands premium prices in developing countries, making it more difficult for recipient firms to get U.S. dollars to pay the donor firm. Many American firms typically insist that all payments be made in American dollars, while many recipient firms wish to pay with their own country's currency. However, in this respect some larger U.S. companies are showing greater flexibility by resorting to barter trade or countertrade as modes of payment.

Equally important issues are the size of the initial fee to be paid to donor firms, the sums to be received as royalties, and how much and how often dividends can be repatriated. If the technology in question is viewed by the recipient government as essential to the country's development, the American donor firm may have more bargaining strength than the recipient firm. This is because in such a situation recipient governments tend to be more flexible. On the other hand, when a nonessential technology is to be imported because of the specific interests of a donor firm, the recipient firm may have greater bargaining strength. In essence, the bargaining strength of the parties depends on their mutual need to make profits, and on the recipient government's needs.

Lengthy Negotiation Periods

Even when governments on both sides have no objections, the gestation period for projects can extend for several months and even years because of a combination of bureaucratic and communications delays. The bureaucracy-related delays in developing countries might consist of delays in seeking licensing, foreign exchange release, approval of search fee and consultant's fee, import license for machinery, and/or raw materials. While it is generally a common ordeal for the recipient firm to deal with its country's bureaucratic structure, it demands a great deal of wisdom and patience from donor firms who are not used to delays that are inexplicable by Western standards.

Poor communication facilities in a developing country can be exasperating to deal with for firms in developed countries. They fail to understand why delivery of mail takes so long (sometimes it may not be delivered), why it is almost impossible to hear clearly over the telephone, or why it takes so long or is sometimes impossible to get a party on the telephone. The efficiency of telegraphic and telex services may be no better. While we can hope for global improvements to ensure effective communication, donor firms may have to send the same message simultaneously through more than one transmission system. This should surely get someone's attention on the other side because repeated failures in communication can, of course, lead to cancellation of contracts and abandonment of projects, however important they may be.

Multiple Influences

More often, officials at various levels deliberately create these hurdles so as to extract "speed-up" money, a way of augmenting their wages. This blatant corruption, rampant in many developing countries, might take decades to eradicate. Meanwhile, business must go on as usual by maneuvering through these barriers.

Political Risks

Few developing nations can claim political stability by Western standards. But, an unstable political environment possesses a greater threat to donor firms with heavy capital investments than to the types of firms and business transactions that are discussed here. Some donors cleverly use this as a ploy to extract more money from the recipients. However, if donor firms feel excessive risk, their investments may be protected by purchasing insurance against political upheaval from federal government sources and private insurance firms.

CATEGORIES OF BARRIERS

The barriers to technology transfer can also be classified into six major categories:

- Political barriers
- Regional barriers
- Social barriers
- Religious barriers
- Ethical barriers
- Economic barriers

Political Barriers

Political barriers include but are not limited to whether or not the recipient country toes the line of the donor nation. The fears of the recipient nation about the donor nation's colonialism movements or aspirations can also become stiff barriers in technology exchange. The fear of colonialism may be real or perceived, but the damage to the transfer process is the same. How does one resolve political misperceptions? Both parties must trust each other and the motives for the transfer.

Regional Barriers

The reason for the formation and existence of regional groups like the European Community (EC) or ASEAN is to promote business and transfer of technology within the countries belonging to the group. So, those who do not belong to the group might not get the same treatment from its members. To reduce this problem, many multinationals have incorporated into separate firms across the world—for example, IBM Brazil, IBM India, and so on.

Social Barriers

Social customs differ from country to country. So, whatever the advantages of a particular technology, unless it fits well with the existing social customs and mores, such technology will not be accepted or used wholeheartedly.

Religious Barriers

Religious differences can prevent flow of technologies from one nation to another due to the incompatibility of religious belief systems, customs, and traditions between donor and recipient countries. For example, McDonald's would not enter the Indian market until it was able to substitute lamb meat for beef in its hamburgers sold in India (the cow is sacred to Hindus, and eating its meat is a violation of their beliefs). Cateora (1983, p. 126) believes that Roman Catholic countries falter commercially because their beliefs about business and economic growth differ from those of Protestant-based economies. He further believes that since both Moslem and Hindu religions stress the irrelevance of temporal life and the importance of future life, these religions often cause barriers to transfer of necessary technologies from other countries which would enable them to achieve rapid economic growth.

Ethical Barriers

Is it ethical to transfer harmful technology to other countries? Inadvertently, firms could transfer technologies that other countries could use for military and destructive purposes.

Economic Barriers

Can the country afford to pay for the technology? If not, who is going to pay for it? A third party like the UN or a philanthropic organization like the Ford Foundation or the government of the donor nation might contribute.

The above barriers may not be entirely eliminated, but they can be overcome by careful planning and execution of the transfer process.

Additional Barriers

Alkhafaji (1995, pp. 252–253) discusses additional problems. The transfer of technology should be without problems to be successful. Many experts have offered reasons as to why the transfers are often unsuccessful. One explanation is the environments of MNCs in developed countries and the environments in which they operate in LDCs. Union Carbide, Bhopal, India, would not have faced a big chemical leak in the mid-1980s, killing thousands of people around the plant, if the work environment had been the same as in the United States. Unfortunately, this is true anywhere; there will always be differences due to the economic and developmental status of the donor and recipient nations. Also, much of the controversy is the result of the different views held by the donor and recipient in terms of goals and objectives, the projected benefits versus costs in the short and long term, the period for completion, and the basic understanding of technological innovation and its diffusion. For instance, LDCs cannot force MNCs to produce technology for LDCs without a sufficient return. More often, technologies developed in advanced countries are not appropriate for developing countries because they do not fit the needs of LDCs and their local conditions. For example, an engineer in a mining company in India convinced the management that it was better to use bullock carts to transport raw material from the mines to a processing center five miles away, rather than mechanized transport. (The costs of replacement parts, repair and maintenance, and fuel were all included in the justification. The uses of bullock carts were cost effective by 3 to 1 against the use of mechanized transport.) But, it would have been difficult for the engineer to convince someone in a foreign country who does not understand how the system in India works, or the different socioeconomic circumstances there. These technological compatibility problems in transfers can be solved only by removing the barriers to compatibility and developing incentives to stimulate the technology transfer process.

Barriers to compatibility are caused by a lack of communication of both the needs and constraints of each party involved during technology transfer. The conflict of interest that occurs in technology transfer pits the profit motive of MNCs against the development needs of LDCs, and MNCs are constrained by the laws of their host countries. Host country constraints have to do with the fact that a host country must try to maximize employment while attempting to balance economic and social advances. When one party does not take the constraints and needs of the other party into account, as often happens, incompatibility results.

Another reason for failure in implementations is that LDCs often do not have the expertise to be able to carry out the technology supplied by MNCs. LDCs often do not have the capability to manage or plan for the new technology. Moreover, they often do not have personnel trained to use the new technology. Further, management is frequently incapable of identifying or resolving problems caused by the new technology.

Another potential obstacle to technology transfer arises when more than the two traditional agents—sender and receiver—are involved. For example, a third party, known as the technology transfer consultant, may be involved. The job of the consultant is to design a system for the transfer that is usually accompanied by the creation of a new plant or the beginning of a new industrial project. This means that a fourth party, such as the engineer of the new building, the builder, or other business people may be involved. As the number of parties involved in an exchange increases, the chance of dispute naturally increases, as does the probability that something will be lost in the exchange of technology.

The major problems in technology transfer can be summarized as follows:

1. Sender and recipient have different views about the process in terms of goals and objectives, expected benefits and costs, period for completion, and general understanding of the technology.

2. MNCs expect a return for their investment. The same technologies are not appropriate for developed countries and LDCs. Some farm equipment cannot be directly transferred because of the tougher grains and plants in LDCs. LDCs often lack trained technicians to service the equipment.

3. Problems can only be solved by removing the barriers to compatibility, which are caused by lack of communication.

4. LDCs may not have the expertise to implement the new technology.

5. The possibility of dispute increases when more than the two traditional agents are involved.

SOLUTIONS

To smooth the process of the transfer, we suggest that first, the donor and recipient countries must be identified and listed on a global level. Second, the technologies available for the transfer and the parties interested in receiving technologies must be collected. Third, a third party organization (a university or educational institution) must supervise and administer the transfer process. This organization keeps track of issues and events.

It is the responsibility of the recipient nation to acknowledge the existence of the barriers. It should evaluate them and take steps to lessen their impact. First, it is important to identify the critical barriers in each transfer situation, identify major players, and analyze their requirements for the transfer process to occur. Second, find an organization that is particularly suited to solve the problem. Third, implement the solution without losing additional time.

In the past, when a barrier existed, a transfer project was often abandoned by both parties—the donor and recipient nations. This process is quite expensive and a waste of time. The author suggests the following mechanisms to remedy the problem:

1. Either the recipient or the donor hires the services of an independent consulting firm to study the situation before the transfer and make recommendations for effective transfer.
2. Recruit an educational institution to help solve the problem.
3. Either party approaches a United Nations agency to seek remedy.
4. Either party approaches government on either side seeking help.
5. Don't take any action and expect the problem will resolve itself over time.

A Success Story

Calcutta's planning experience after independence is noteworthy for two reasons: First, it included an unprecedented effort at transferring Western planning technology (mainly through the Ford Foundation) to a Third World city; second, it serves as a graphic example of how the larger picture of a city's future is drawn by forces of politics and economics. Using Calcutta's story as the background, this chapter has examined the issues involved in transfer of planning technology (diffusion, permanence, etc.) and the overwhelming importance of the political economy of the receiving region in deciding acceptance or rejection of the transfer, and in shaping subsequent urban development.

CONCLUSION

Major barriers to technology transfer to Third World countries are identified and solutions to these barriers discussed. This calls for the DCs to devote additional time to the economic growth problems of the poor and less developed Third World nations. The DCs should take the initiative. They should create and transfer relevant or appropriate technologies to these developing countries with missionary zeal. Otherwise, proper transfer may not happen. Also, special attention must be given to implementation. Important issues include organizational problems, identifying a commercial sponsor, appointing a team to achieve the transfer, and building transfer mechanisms into the plan. Planners, markets, and production people are important participants in the process (Cravens 1994, p. 85).

Chapter Four

Ethical Dimensions

This chapter explores the issues related to global business ethics in technology transfer. It will address the economic and environmental issues, and human rights issues and their effect on technology transfer in the global marketplace. Examples from three Third World countries (Thailand, Indonesia, and China) are given. Finally, in discussing how international firms should address the ethical dilemmas, Laczniak and Murphy's (1991) ethical checklist for a global marketplace is adapted.

In an age of increasing globalization of business, a new perspective for evaluating business ethics is warranted. This new perspective should consider the multiple religious, ethnic, and cultural perspectives that prevail in the modern business world rather than rely on traditional Judeo-Christian ethics alone.

The need for global business ethics is particularly important in the area of technology transfers that happen among various countries. As technology moves from one country to another, ethical concerns relating to environment and economy arise. For example, human rights issues are a major concern for Western nations in dealing with international exchanges and relationships. Many ethical dilemmas crop up in technology transfers between the United States and Taiwan, Thailand, Indonesia, and China. Issues concerning pollution, job creation, piracy, human rights policies, and corruption are constantly arising. Also, questions arise concerning the legitimacy of the benefits of technology transfer versus the ethical responsibility that each country should have in the technology transfer process. To resolve these issues, we need some common ethical framework or guidelines that all participating countries could understand and would be willing to abide by. This chapter deals with multiple aspects of global business ethics and technology transfer. It includes revising Laczniak and Murphy's (1991) ethical guidelines to be part of a framework for global business ethics.

Concern for global business ethics is growing, and this subject is sparsely treated in the literature. Over the past twenty years, interest in ethical issues, such as in international business, has grown immensely as the public has become more aware of and concerned about both potential and actual business abuses (Dubinsky and Loken 1989). Perhaps this concern with business ethics could also be due to countless incidents and events where ethics was the central issue, such as Watergate or the Vietnam War (Armstrong et al. 1990, p. 5). Marketers and members of other business disciplines are particularly subject to ethical considerations in doing their job functions (Cohen, Pant, and Sharp 1993, p. 14). Furthermore, much of the criticism about ethical behavior in business is aimed at marketing (Goolsby and Hunt 1992) because marketing people are usually the final links between a business and its customers, suppliers, channel members, competition, the public, and other stakeholders.

Ethical issues in marketing often revolve around the issues of bribery, fairness, honesty, pricing, product, personnel, confidentiality, advertising, manipulation of data, and purchasing (Chonko and Hunt 1985). Armstrong (1992) suggests the following ethical problems in international business: bribery, inappropriate products or technology, tax evasion practices, illegal or immoral activities, questionable commissions to channel members, and involvement in cultural and political affairs. Cultural differences among nations have created new problems that may not be addressed when operating domestically. Economic and environmental impacts on host countries, along with human rights issues, must be considered when engaging in technology transfer.

ETHICS DEFINED

Ethics has different meanings to different people depending on their religious, ethnic, and cultural belief systems and backgrounds. Some people consider any action as ethical when it is legal. Some assume that ethics is a fixed set of standards and rules that everyone must follow (Ulrich and Thielmann 1993, p. 879). Bartels (1967, p. 21) defines ethics as the standard by which business actions may be judged as right or wrong. Ferrell and Fraedrich (1991, p. 4) offer that ethics is the study and philosophy of human conduct, with an emphasis on the determination of right and wrong. Finally, Tsalikis and Fritzsche (1989) use the term "ethics" interchangeably with "morals." Amba Rao defines ethics as "the moral thinking and analysis by corporate decision makers and other members, regarding the motives and consequences of their decisions and actions" (1993, p. 555). This definition is more precise because it includes the motives and consequences of decisions and allows that a solitary standard or rule cannot be applied to distinct situations. In a similar vain, Bartels (1967) emphasizes that ethics is a concern for people, not just acts or things, and that business is primarily a social process within an economic process with marketing being a specialized process involving role relationships and interactions. Ferrell and Weaver (1978) also suggest that the impact of social interaction on ethical behavior within the firm is a major consideration in understanding ethical behavior.

Business ethics requires that an organization or individual behave to meet the rules of moral philosophy (Robin and Reidenback 1987). Corporations usually have corporate codes of ethics; however, such codes have been directed more toward issues that affect the "bottom line" (internal to the firm) than toward the interests of society (Robin and Reidenbach 1987). Ferrell and Gresham (1985) suggest that the pressure for profit may sometimes cause ethics to be overlooked. It is often difficult to discuss ethical constraints in business because there is no single standard by which actions can be judged as ethical or unethical. Among marketing managers there is a lack of consensus regarding what is ethical conduct (Ferrell and Gresham 1985) both within a country and globally.

Laczniak summarizes proposals for ethical standards made by various marketing writers (Peter and Donnelly 1995, p. 260):

1. *The Golden Rule*: A person should act in a way that he/she would want others to act toward him/her;

2. *The Utilitarian Principle*: A person should act in a way that provides the greatest good for the greatest number of people;

3. *Kant's Categorical Imperative*: A person should act in a way so that the action taken under the circumstances could be a rule of behavior;

4. *The Professional Ethic*: A person should take actions that would be viewed as proper by a distinguished panel of colleagues in that particular field; and

5. *The T.V. Test*: A person should ask him or herself: "Would I feel comfortable explaining my actions to a national T.V. audience?"

Thus, although ethics is difficult to define, and although it is equally difficult to apply a fixed set of standards to all situations, ethical decisions still need to be made that impact a firm in addition to one or more countries. In business, especially international business, unique situations arise that require prompt resolutions. Unprecedented situations require the ability to adapt and change the process of decision making. Ulrich and Thielmann suggest that we should not ask whether managers are ethical, but what kind of thinking pattern they have developed to legitimize their actions within the sphere òf the debate between ethics and economic success, both for their own peace of mind and for others (1993, p. 880).

CULTURAL DIFFERENCES

A major ethical problem facing American managers in international business is cultural difference (Armstrong et al. 1990). What may be considered ethical behavior to an American executive may be considered abhorrent by a particular culture. Similarly, the practices of many cultures are considered shameful by Americans. Ethical decision making in other countries is thought to be influenced by culture (Cohen, Pant, and Sharp 1993, p. 12). Managers of companies who do business abroad must be aware of these differences and have a better understanding of culture-based diversities before entering into foreign markets (Armstrong et al. 1990).

Therefore, following a set of ethics in global business can be a difficult task because of cultural and other differences that exist among and between diverse nations. Hunt and Vitell (1986), in their model, offer that the first step is the perception of an ethical problem. Additionally, they offer that cultural environment, industry environment, organizational environment, and personal experiences can influence the background factors in ethical decision making. Reidenbach and Robin (1988) suggest that these conflicting ideas, rules, and interpretations may lead to conflicting evaluations of what is right and wrong.

The cultural differences between countries will definitely have impact if an action is perceived as an ethical issue by either or both of the countries involved. Some argue that there is a direct correlation between ethical behavior and the level of economic development of a country because the legal systems in these countries are not as advanced and/or the social expectations are not as high (Amba Rao 1993, p. 555).

Although ethics varies across geographic borders, a dilemma arises when a multinational corporation must decide whether it should adapt its ethical policies to those of the host country, or whether it should try to influence the host country to change its ethical standards to match those of the corporation's home country. A leading question is whether more developed countries who are transferring technologies to underdeveloped countries should attempt to transfer ethical standards as well. Amba Rao suggests that the host government should control a multinational corporation's behavior and the multinational corporation should respect the traditions and laws of the host nation. Additionally, the host government should respect the multinational corporation and provide a climate for growth (1993, p. 559).

THE ENVIRONMENT

Americans have long been concerned with the environment and its impact on future generations. Several public service announcements appeal to Americans to recycle to reduce waste and save the ozone layer. Factories must follow regulations concerning emissions and dumping procedures. Efforts to "Keep America Beautiful" and reduce the level of toxins in the air and water supplies have been made to control the pollution and contamination. Americans look to protect the environment, which they hope will provide a safe and comfortable dwelling place for future generations.

Although Americans place a high priority on investing in the environment, ethical issues have been raised concerning American companies' responsibility toward the environments of the nations to which technology is being transferred. When these recipients of technology transfer are unwilling to accept environmental responsibility, should American companies intervene? Also, should American companies follow American environmental standards when operating abroad, or should they conform to the perhaps lower standards of the host countries' governments?

For example, over the past 40 years, Taiwan has undergone an economic transformation that has gained the country the position as the world's twelfth largest trader. The annual per capita income in Taiwan is the second highest in Asia (Sheng, Chang, and French 1994, p. 887). However, this newfound wealth has brought serious problems to Taiwan. Taipei has one of the highest pollution indexes in the world; it rates more than double that of a smoggy day in Los Angeles (Sheng, Chang, and French 1994, p. 887). The Taiwanese government has promised money and new regulations in response to concerns over effects of rapid economic growth on the environment (Sheng, Chang, and French 1994, p. 896).

What does this mean to American businesses setting up operations in Taiwan? First, U.S. companies must decide their own standards regarding pollution and the environment in relation to how the Taiwanese feel about environmental issues. They must decide whether to follow the regulations of the Taiwanese government (if these regulations are less stringent than those of the U.S. government) or to apply their own standards to the foreign operations. The question is whether it is ethical for American companies to operate in a way that is detrimental to the environment of a foreign country simply because that country's environmental standards are not as high. An American firm must be prepared to face scrutiny from American activist groups and activists in Taiwan if it chooses to ignore strict American standards and operate according to lower standards.

Some may argue that the United States should not be responsible for Taiwan's lack of sufficient regulations concerning the environment and pollution. The Taiwanese are not as concerned and motivated by their moral judgment and perceptions of what is right or wrong as they are by achieving gain and harmony simultaneously (Sheng, Chang, and French 1994, p. 896). If this is the case, some may feel that as long as U.S. companies operate according to the Taiwanese standards, their ethical and moral responsibilities are fulfilled. Consequently, should the people of Taiwan suffer, it is solely the responsibility of the Taiwanese.

On the other hand, it can be argued that the American firm is responsible if it violates business ethics, even when it is operating in another country that may not care much about the ethical standards. Therefore, it would be unethical for U.S. companies to lower their standards when operating in foreign lands. Some hold the belief that imposing American values on host countries helps promote ethical behavior that can become an example to other countries (Amba Rao 1993, p. 560). Some believe that it is the responsibility of American companies that are familiar with causes and problems of pollution, for instance, to convey that knowledge to the countries in which they do business and transfer technology.

TECHNOLOGY TRANSFER AND ECONOMIC GROWTH

Technology transfers create economic impact not only on the country that is receiving the transfer, but also on the country that is providing the technology, because of reverse technology benefits. Okoroafo believes that "recently liberalized environments provide greater export opportunities for products previously protected by government policies" (1993, p. 185). However, the economic impact of technology transfer can be positive or negative for both participants in the transfer. The economic impact of technology transfer gives birth to ethical dilemmas encountered by both countries.

Multinational corporations constantly move operations from one country to another in search of low labor costs, among other things. A multinational corporation can often find overseas locations that can produce its goods and services more cheaply than its U.S. plants. Some argue that this arrangement is beneficial to the multinational corporation, but it weakens the host country's government because the multinational corporation does not reinvest its labor savings into that country's local infrastructure (Sethi 1993, p. 10). Others argue that although technology transfers claim to offer jobs to the needy citizens of the host country, employment is not really given to new workers; rather, positions are filled by workers already employed by the company or workers who are hired away from similar companies in the area. For ins ance, Pepsi pulled out of South Africa in 1985 and went back in 1994 when the black majority won the right to elect its own government. When Pepsi returned, it became a symbol of black economic power and instilled hope in the citizens that new jobs would be created for them. However, South Africans got angry with Pepsi because they felt that it was not hiring the neediest people and training them. Instead, Pepsi was taking experienced workers from Coca-Cola and other already established companies (Keller 1994, A4). In cases such as this, technology transfer is seen only as widening the gap between the rich and the poor (Amba Rao 1993, p. 557).

While some believe that technology transfer harms more than helps a receiving nation, others argue that it is truly beneficial to the developing nation. Developing nations need technology transfer to catch up to the rest of the developed world. Technology transfer serves to modernize these economies so that they can compete in the world market (Shelp et al. 1984, p. 9). The positive effects of technology transfer, such as industrial growth, skill development, and increased managerial abilities are sometimes considered to far outweigh the negative effects (Amba Rao 1993, p. 557). Countries such as Taiwan have experienced tremendous growth over the years due to technology transfer. These countries, many of which have high poverty rates, rely on the growth benefits of technology transfer to eliminate poverty and gain a share of the global market.

While nations such as the United States experience cost-saving benefits from technology transfers, they also do experience some serious consequences. First, when an American company gets involved with a developing nation that is going through political and social struggles, the economic performance of that firm may suffer. For example, when Pepsi went back to South Africa, it identified very closely with the cause of the South African blacks. Pepsi may have given the impression that it is not a business, but rather a social program (Keller 1994, p. A4). When a company gets too involved in the struggles of a foreign country, it may limit itself to a particular market and run the risk of diluting its earnings by placing a higher priority on social agendas than profits.

Another problem faced by nations that transfer technology is copyright infringements by the developing nation. Countries and companies who transfer technology run the risk of having their products illegally copied. For example, the Chinese have been copying U.S. products such as software, music, and movies, and they do not seem to see anything wrong with doing this (Post and Strasser 1995). This poses a threat to U.S. companies who export their goods to China because the value of the goods decreases when "knock-offs" become available. However, China's is the fastest growing economy in the world, and some U.S. businesses feel that this market is worth the risk because the future rewards are expected to be great. As a result, U.S. firms invested over $2 billion in China in 1993 (Post and Strasser 1995).

Ethical implications arise when discussing economic impacts of technology transfer, from the viewpoints of both the developing nation and the developed nation. First, ethical considerations lie in the "payback" of the developing nations to the provider of the technology. There exists the possibility of exploiting the underdeveloped nations by luring them with technology and economic growth. Second, the possibility of piracy and copyright infringement by the receiving company exists, as proven by China's behavior toward the United States. While Americans feel that this is considered theft and extremely unethical, the Chinese see nothing wrong with it. Some Chinese officials have said that U.S. companies should be flattered that the Chinese liked their products well enough to copy them (Post and Strasser 1995). Here, cultural differences play a role in the perception of what is ethical and what is unethical; regardless, the economic impact of these decisions and actions is significant.

HUMAN RIGHTS ISSUES

The United States considers itself a "civilized" nation. Although many in this country may have their own complaints, no one can deny that U.S. workers are treated far more humanely than workers in other nations. In the United States, regulations exist concerning how little a worker can be paid and the conditions in which a worker is expected to do his or her job. Americans frown upon those nations accused of exploiting their workers for the sake of money. We cringe at the thought of women and children slaving in foreign factories earning less in a day than we do in an hour, yet we buy the very products that these women and children toil over.

When American companies engage in technology transfer with countries who do not have the same philosophies about human rights as Americans do, the American company faces an ethical dilemma. The company, whether or not it practically promotes those activities, is linked to those activities. The company must decide whether it will take a stand and demand that the country engage in some kind of reform, or whether it will, as the old adage says, "do as the Romans do."

Where does this leave American companies who are engaged in technology transfer with countries whose human rights policies are less developed than those of America? Some feel multinational corporations should play a role in the growth, technology transfer, and improvement of living standards of other nations (Sethi 1993, p. 11). What are U.S. companies to do, however, if these countries do not adopt the same principles that Americans have? Pulling out of these countries would result in enormous financial losses for both the American business and the host country. Also, some may argue that it would be unethical to cease operations in a foreign country and deny that country valuable technology simply because the government will not conform to the standards set in America. This would have doubly severe impact on individual citizens because not only would they be subject to inhumane treatment, but they would also continue to live in poverty with less opportunity to escape it.

However, companies operating in countries where human rights are violated suffer too. These companies are subject to the scrutiny of the people in the country in which they are operating. This can mean financial losses on both ends. If the citizens of the host country feel that American companies promote this behavior, negative feelings may result and the company may not be successful in that particular country. Also, if Americans find out that a company is engaging in transfers with countries notorious for treating people inhumanely, boycotts and negative publicity may result, in which the company suffers a blow to its reputation, and lost revenues.

American companies face these dilemmas today. The following section of this chapter will focus specifically on the U.S. relationship with three countries: Thailand, Indonesia, and China, and the ethical implications surrounding this relationship with these countries, whose human rights policies are questionable.

Thailand

Working conditions in Thailand would be considered slavish in the United States. Thailand's official daily minimum wage is $5.20 (McNulty 1994, p. 16A). It is not unusual for a Thai worker to work thirteen hours a day and earn only $5 plus a certain amount of change for each overtime hour. In some Thai factories, laborers have been chained and beaten. A Thai worker considers the working conditions to be good if he or she works in a factory that is clean, brightly lit, and air conditioned (McNulty 1994, p. 16A).

Factory workers in Thailand assemble anything from clothing to Mighty Morphin Power Rangers. Most of these workers cannot even afford to buy the products they assemble. For example, Mighty Morphin Power Rangers that cost about $13.50 in the United States sell in Bangkok for $88 each (McNulty 1994, p. 16A). At $5.20 per day, it would take a Thai worker about three weeks just to earn enough money to pay for the fruits of his/her labor.

In Thailand, the ethical question that arises is whether U.S. businesses should support these labor standards by setting up operations there. One must consider, however, that although working conditions are poor, technology transfer does provide a benefit to this country. Without foreign investment and operations in this country, workers may not have the opportunity to be employed and earn a minimum wage. Technology transfer provides the means for a nation to grow and to improve living standards; however, growth and improvement take time. Some may reason that these conditions are acceptable for the time being until substantial growth and attainment of global competitive advantage are realized. After all, there was a time in history when the United States participated in unfair and harsh labor practices as well.

Indonesia

Companies such as Nike, Reebok, and Levi Strauss look to countries such as Indonesia in search of cheap labor (Goodman 1993, p. 26). In Indonesia, the labor is cheap, and it is not uncommon for an Indonesian to work 60 hours per week in a hot, poorly ventilated factory and make only the equivalent of $1.28 per day. Officials in Indonesia say that these wages must stay low to maintain Indonesia's competitive advantage over other countries. These low wages attract foreign investment, which is the key to job creation and growth. Growth is the key to wiping out poverty (Goodman 1993, p. 26).

Human rights advocates say that poverty and poor living conditions are not solely attributable to market forces. They feel that Indonesia's business community, government, and military conspire to keep wealth from reaching those who create it (Goodman 1993, p. 27). Few laborers realize how much profit their labor is bringing their employers. Many do not even know that there is a minimum wage. The laborers do not seem to be receiving any of the wealth generated. Those who do see what is going on feel powerless to do anything about it (Goodman 1993, p. 28).

Like Thailand, Indonesia experiences the benefit of growth from technology transfer; however, the problem with Indonesia seems to lie with a corrupt government. A leading ethical question here is whether American companies and American government should be a force in assuring that the wealth is seen by all, not just by the government, military, and business sectors. Also, American companies must consider whether they are willing to be associated with a country that exploits its workers, allowing the rich to get richer while the poor continue to be oppressed.

China

China is on an upward growth trend. China has the world's fourth largest economy, which is becoming increasingly market-driven and consumer-oriented (Heenan 1993, p. 35). Given China's enormous population, one might guess that it has a vast labor pool. The People's Republic of China has more than 20 percent of the world's population and a workforce of around 580 million (Heenan 1993, p. 36). Many multinational corporations are looking to China because of its growth in technical talent. China educates more scientists and engineers than France and Germany combined (Heenan 1993, p. 36). However, China has gained a reputation for being an inhumane society. It cracks down on political and religious dissenters, as exemplified by the Tienanmen Square Massacre in 1989.

Yet China's most favored trading partner status with the United States was renewed by President Clinton in 1994, which has caused mixed feelings among Americans and Chinese alike because of the controversies surrounding China's stance on human rights. Some feel that although China signed the International Declaration of Human Rights, it has failed to abide by it (Desruisseaux 1994, p. A30). Clinton made China's improvement on human rights the basis for renewing tariff privileges in the U.S. market, but some feel that China has shown that it has no intention of making serious progress in human rights (Lizhi and Haiching 1994, p. A27).

China's government is seen as corrupt. Whereas Indonesia and Thailand are accused of mistreating their workers, China is accused of mistreating its citizens in general. The U.S. government and U.S. companies are feeling the pressures of being economically and technologically associated with this nation. President Clinton has faced criticism for renewing China's trade status with the United States. Some are angry because they feel that China will not improve on human rights without outside pressure (Desruisseaux 1994, p. A30). Others feel that the economic benefits of trading with China are just too good to pass up. Still others have mixed feelings, arguing that Clinton should revoke the most favored trading nation status for products made or sold by government-controlled enterprises, but should not cancel them for the private sector, which needs to grow (Lizhi and Haiching 1994, p. A27).

IMPACT ON CULTURE

Technology transfer has a significant impact on culture. If one reflects back to the state of this country 100 years ago, technology obviously played a key role in its growth and development. New technologies not only affect our businesses, they also affect our daily lives.

Ethical questions arise when countries like the United States transfer technologies to nations that may not be ready for this growth or have no obvious need for this new technology (such as the Mighty Morphin Power Rangers discussed earlier in this chapter). One may wonder who can afford these expensive toys. Some may argue that there is no need for Mighty Morphin Power Rangers in Bangkok, but that this is simply a tactic to try to "Americanize" the country and exploit it through an attempt to create demand for useless American products. Some critics may argue that technology transfer to Third World countries simply serves as a way to control these countries and make them dependent on things deemed important by the transferring nation.

A FRAMEWORK

In addressing the variety of ethical dilemmas that exist in technology transfer, we can consider Laczniak and Murphy's (1991) series of eight questions to address whether contemplated actions are ethical or possibly have ethical consequences, as shown below. This checklist of eight questions can be extended to address the ethical issues for both the host country and the multinational business.

1. Does the contemplated action violate law?
   a. In the multinational firm's home country?
   b. In the host country?
2. Is the contemplated action contrary to widely accepted moral obligations?
   a. In the multinational firm's home country?
   b. In the host country?
   c. As perceived by global human rights organizations?
3. Does the proposed action violate any other special obligations that stem from the type of marketing organization at focus?
   a. In the multinational firm's home country?
   b. In the host country?
   c. Are basic human rights being violated?
4. Is the intent of the contemplated action harmful?
   a. To the stockholders in the multinational firm?
   b. To the customers of the multinational firm both in the home country and abroad?
   c. To the citizens of the home and/or host country?
5. Are there any major damages to people or organizations that are likely to result from the contemplated action?
   a. In the multinational firm's home country?
   b. In the host country?
6. Is there a satisfactory alternative action which produces equal or greater benefits to all the parties affected than the proposed action?

   a. That respects the law and culture of the multinational firm's home country?

   b. That respects the law and culture of the host country?

7. Does the contemplated action infringe upon the inalienable rights of the consumer as well as the worker who created the product?

   a. In the multinational firm's home country?

   b. In other countries that are involved through either the production, marketing, and/or consumption of the product?

8. Does the proposed action leave another person or group less well off? Is this person or group already a member of a relatively underprivileged class?

   a. In the multinational firm's home country?

   b. In the host country?

   c. Is there something the firm could do to improve the relative standing of this less well off or underprivileged person or group that would not seriously violate its obligations to its other stakeholders?

In applying this extension of Laczniak and Murphy's ethical checklist, we propose that multinational firms can make a positive impact in some ways on the environment and human rights in other countries without violating those countries' cultural beliefs, such as providing education, meals, and clean and safe working conditions to their Third World employees. We are not advocating trying to change another country's laws or cultural beliefs, but instead offer that multinational firms cannot use that as an excuse to ignore blatant human rights and environmental violations. In fact, ignoring these violations, while legal in the host country, may affect how that firm's home consumers and stakeholders view them (i.e., horrendous working conditions in a Third World plant may impact consumers' purchase of that product in America). Sturdivant and Ginter (1977) offer evidence that suggests that ethically responsible firms do enjoy better economic performance. Furthermore, Robin and Reidenbach (1987, p. 52) illustrate how a firm can integrate ethical and social responsibility into its strategic marketing plan through: (1) providing an ethical profile as part of the mission statement that guides the development of marketing objectives, (2) identifying all the impacted publics, (3) developing ethical core values for the firm that affect its development of the marketing mix, (4) integrating these core values into the firm's organizational culture, and (5) monitoring both the marketing and ethical effectiveness. Thus, we propose that ethical decision making can still go hand-in-hand with technology transfer in Third World countries such as Thailand, Indonesia, and China without violating those countries' cultural beliefs.

We illustrate how this process for global ethical decision making, in the case of technology transfer, using Laczniak and Murphy's guidelines, would look in Figure 4.1. This figure illustrates that each of the countries

Figure 4.1
A Global Ethical Framework for Evaluating Technology Transfer

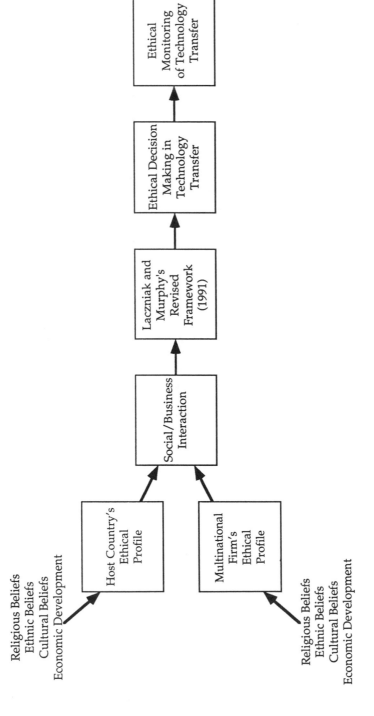

involved can first be seen as having an ethical profile (as addressed for a firm by Robin and Reidenbach 1987) that is based on their religious, ethnic, and cultural beliefs (Cohen, Pant, and Sharp 1993) as well as economic development (Amba Rao 1993). The ethical profile of one country (either the host or the multinational firm's home country) interacts with the other in both a social and business sense. This interaction is a key concept in both Ferrell and Weaver's (1978) and Bartels's (1967) discussion of ethics. We propose that this interaction needs to consider our global updating of Laczniak and Murphy's ethical checklist prior to any ethical decision making. Finally, per Robin and Reidenbach (1987) it is important for the multinational firm to monitor its ethical decisions, in terms of both the multinational firm's home country and the host country. We feel that through consideration of these ethical profiles and global ethical checklist, and with continual monitoring, ethical decisions in the area of technology transfer that are ethical for all parties involved are more likely to be made.

CONCLUSION

By creating economic impacts on the participating nations, companies also create many ethical dilemmas to both host and recipient nations. Therefore, multinational corporations that offer technologies and host governments that receive technology should consider ethical aspects in their decision making, as well as the economic aspects (Amba Rao, 1993).

However, a major problem facing international businesses today is coping with diverse cultures across geographic borders where ethics are defined differently around the globe. This creates a challenge to companies in not only deciding what they feel is ethical, but also in determining the ethical standards of the host country. This is usually not a problem when the standards of both countries are nearly similar, such as with Canada and the United States. The real problem starts when the host country's ethics are much lower than those of the American company.

When an American firm decides to have business relationships with companies in developing nations, the American company must decide whether to operate according to its own ethical standards or to lower its standards to fit that of the host company. Some feel that as long as the multinational corporation abides by the laws and customs of the host country, then its responsibility is fulfilled. This raises some interesting questions. First, how can a company consider its ethical responsibility fulfilled when it operates with different standards in different countries? Also, if a company operates according to the ethical standards set by the country in which it operates, then is the company really being an ethical force, or is it simply being a conformist?

These questions are difficult to answer because different people have different ideas about what is ethical behavior. Some see ethical behavior as a clear black-and-white issue, while others argue that moral reasoning is influenced by environmental factors and individual characteristics (Goolsby and Hunt 1992). To help address these questions, we have extended the ethical checklist of Laczniak and Murphy (1991) and illustrated this in Figure 4.1 to better address the ethical issues of multinational firms in the area of technology transfer. Questions about what is ethical or unethical will perhaps never be fully clarified. If American companies refuse to claim responsibility for the actions of the countries in which they operate, then they must be prepared to accept responsibility for their own ethical actions, especially in terms of responses by their own consumers and stockholders. Thus, these companies must realize that their actions affect not only Americans and their firm's profit margin, but also the environment, economy, and culture of the nations they do business with.

Chapter Five

A Model of Technology Transfer Assimilation

To achieve maximum benefit, transferred technologies should be assimilated properly into the host country's socioeconomic and cultural fabric. Otherwise, it is a wasted effort. This chapter suggests a model useful for the proper assimilation of transferred technologies. The model is based on certain basic assumptions. Traditionally, MNCs and DCs have held all the prerogatives in technology transfer. For instance, the donors of technology would decide what type of technology they would transfer, to whom, when, how much, and at what price. Firms in LDCs or their governments did not have much say in these matters. However, due to increasing competition today to expand into the growing LDC and emerging Eastern European markets, this situation is gradually changing and the host or receiving nations can bargain with the donors better than before.

THE MODEL

The components of the model, as shown in Figure 5.1, consist of donors, recipients, technology, and the process of transfer in a global environment concerned with ecological, ethical, cultural, economic, and security considerations.

Donors

Typically, the donors of technology are the firms located in DCs. These can be private, public, or jointly owned by both the public and private organizations. Most of the technology transfers are made by MNCs like

Figure 5.1
Technology Transfer Assimilation Model

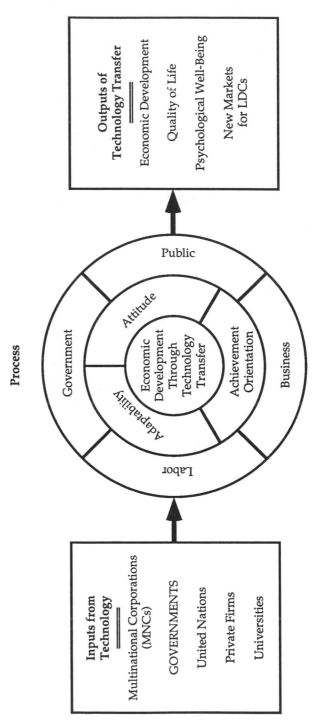

Coca-Cola, Toyota, BMW, and the like that constantly keep expanding their operations worldwide to gain new markets for their products.

Recipients

The recipients or host nations are usually private or public firms in LDCs that would want new technologies in the hope that such new technologies can enhance their incomes, either through domestic and/or export marketing. Recipients are also willing to pay premium prices for certain technologies that they can use in producing goods that have high profit margins (popular consumer products, cosmetics, and household cleaning chemicals, for example).

Environmental Variables

Ethical Considerations. Often, donor firms are concerned about the ethical impact that technology transfer will have on the donor nation. Due to lack of supervision and regular monitoring by the donor, major disasters such as the one Union Carbide's Bhopal plant had in India could happen again. The chemical leaks in Bhopal in 1985 killed and seriously injured tens of thousands of people living within two miles around the plant's location.

Ecological Considerations. In the same vein, an operation that could potentially cause water and air pollution in a big way or depletes available natural resources like trees, as in the lumber industry, comes under the category of ecological scrutiny.

Cultural Considerations. In transferring technology to other countries, companies must be aware of cultural differences between the donor and recipient nation. Technologies can fail in other countries if they do not fit the host nation's culture. For example, a scheme to market infant milk in Brazil failed because most mothers there breast-feed their children.

Religious Considerations. Religion plays a vital role in the lives of people in most developing countries. As described in Chapter 3, Hindus worship the cow; therefore, they do not eat beef. So, McDonald's would operate in India by offering lamburgers instead of traditional hamburgers made out of beef patties. As most Indians are vegetarians, vegetarian patties made out of the soybean or potato can be substituted for the meat.

Levels of Education. Education is the key to a successful career in LDCs and even in DCs, for that matter. In developing countries, the literacy rate usually is low—about 30 percent overall. Technology transfer cannot be successful if the host country's education levels and literacy rates are poor.

METHODS OF TRANSFER

Major methods of transfer were discussed earlier. Joint venture, licensing, wholly owned subsidiary, management contract, and turnkey operations are some popular methods of transfer. A popular method of technology transfer today is joint venture. It is closely followed by franchising with the proliferation of franchises like McDonald's, Holiday Inn, and so on throughout the world. Some older technologies are sold at lump sum as a one-time sale. Newer technologies are sold through complex arrangements including a combination of up-front fee, royalty, purchase of raw materials from the donor, management training fee, and so on.

THE TRANSFER PROCESS

Today, the Internet makes it easy to access the publicly available information and documents. Considerable technology, particularly in software, also gets disseminated in this manner. But manufacturing and consulting technology requires closer supervision, as they are people-oriented transfers.

ASSIMILATION

As stated before, transferred technologies fail unless they are properly assimilated into the host country's socioeconomic life. This leads to enormous waste of resources and loss of valuable time. Also, many developing countries can leapfrog into advanced technologies because of the availability of unique human resources. Thus, Bangalore, India, for example, has become a software center in the last decade because of the availability of low-cost programmers in India in general, and Bangalore in particular. So, major computer firms like IBM, Hewlett-Packard, and so on have set up software manufacturing subsidiaries there. Newly developed software can be beamed via satellite to the U.S. headquarters for further processing and for domestic and worldwide marketing.

TECHNOLOGY TRANSFER AND ECONOMIC GROWTH

Also, to achieve rapid economic growth, like Japan or the four tigers in Southeast Asia (Hong Kong, Singapore, Taiwan, and South Korea), countries should have a basic economic growth model different from the input-output models and other econometrics models. A new behavioral model for economic growth is postulated. According to this model, people in LDCs should emulate the success of Japan and other Pacific Basin NICs. They should first develop and sustain the core characteristics of proper attitude, achievement orientation, and adaptation. They should have positive attitudes and develop achievement orientation. Also, they should be flexible to quickly adapt a given technology to meet their unique needs instead of direct copying. In the case of Japan, these core behavioral characteristics were greatly enhanced by the opportune environment—public loyalty to Japanese goods and businesses, heavy government support to business including low-interest loans, sympathetic labor unions, and profit-sharing businesses. Finally, following World War II, Japan was also blessed with an international environment that demanded low-cost, high-quality imports regardless of where they came from. With its aggressive export-push strategy, Japan did take advantage of this opportunity to gain large market shares in global markets in products ranging from automobiles to cameras.

THE CHALLENGES

There are quite a few challenges for nations receiving technologies. What good is technology transfer unless it is absorbed and assimilated well into the sociocultural fabric of the host country? What good is technology transfer unless the host country is able to put it to use for enhancing national wealth through exports, as Japan and other successful Pacific Basin countries did? What good is technology transfer unless it brings the host country in par with other developed countries in terms of economic status, at least in the long run? To answer these questions, a modified version of an earlier behavioral growth model developed by me and my colleagues is presented here (Reddy, Oliver, Rao, and Addington 1984).

According to this model, the inflow of technologies has to be properly integrated into the society of a developed country by adopting the integrated behavioral model as the core structure. For example, when the Japanese borrowed concepts of photocopying or making computer chips they not only were able to absorb such technology quickly but also were able to integrate these technologies into various products that they manufacture in Japan. Thus, computer chips are used in a variety of Japanese products from cameras to industrial drilling machinery. And borrowed technology leads to original plus newer products. This feature of customization of technology to suit each country is extremely important to countries that are currently on the far end of the economic growth spectrum, that is, very poor.

Presumably, other countries may not possess the behavioral characteristics of the Japanese people or be able to achieve similar economic growth. But, the model can be modified to fit each country's unique sociocultural-religious-economic-ethics background.

The integrated macro-behavioral model has been developed to provide a better understanding of the key forces underlying the Japanese economic miracle rather than to suggest decisive policy formulas for others to follow the Japanese path to economic progress. This model is based on a certain key assumption: that a nation, however resource-poor it may be, by modifying or fine-tuning the existing behavioral traits of the people, can lead the country to desired goals—in this case, economic achievement. Also, a successful blend of necessary behavioral traits with the coalition of certain internal and external favorable circumstances can produce a synergistic effect. Countries experiencing a "vicious cycle of poverty" are going through negative synergies. For example, unless the quality of their product is improved, exports will not improve, but to improve quality, they need the profits from the export markets so that they can reinvest in better manufacturing equipment and employee training. By maintaining "relationship marketing" with other countries, a developing country can improve its bargaining position in export markets, or for that matter, in acquiring new technologies from DCs.

The model as described in Figure 5.1 is behavioral and integrated in character in that it focuses on the critical behavioral characteristics that serve as the catalytic agents for the Japanese economic success. These behavioral traits are: Japanese attitude, their achievement orientation, and their adaptability. These three core variables, constantly interacting with each other and sometimes overlapping, pervade the gamut of the Japanese economy (government, business, labor, and public), further aided by two facilitating environmental factors: the "import-pull" and "export-push" factors. As a result of their constant interaction, a synergistic effect is created.

As a conceptual model, the important merit of the model is its parsimonious nature. It integrates various behavioral and social and economic factors. Although this oversimplification might limit its general application, especially to countries that possess drastically different socioeconomic backgrounds compared with Japan, the model, nonetheless, could be useful to many nations in understanding the true nature of the Japanese economic success. Another limitation of the model is that it has not been empirically tested and is based purely on a synthesis of the currently available literature and opinions expressed by well-known writers in the field.

Attitudes

Attitude may be defined as the general predisposition of people toward any object including themselves, family, nation, and world. How do the Japanese differ from others? How do their attitudes relate to economic success?

The Japanese are a homogeneous society, speak one language, have two major religions (Shintoism and Buddhism), are family oriented, are very patriotic, revere authority, are frugal and hardworking, and possess the "Samurai spirit" (esprit de corps).

The Japanese differ from the rest of the world in the intensity with which they hold attitudes. For instance, G. W. England (1975) found Japanese managers to be more pragmatic, warmer, and less moralistic than their U.S., Korean, Australian, and Indian counterparts. Japanese managers also attach greater importance to organizational goals, especially high productivity, growth, long-run profit maximization, stability, and industry leadership. The most relevant personal goals of the managers were achievement and creativity, while they expressed less concern for job satisfaction and dignity. In their association with people, Japanese managers oddly scored on loyalty, honor, trust, tolerance, and obedience while placing a high value on aggressiveness. Perhaps this is because a general lack of aggressiveness in the society makes aggression a scarce and, therefore, highly valued behavior.

In his study of twelve national groupings of successful managers, Bass (1979) described the Japanese as wanting to be objective, persistent, proactive, and long-term in outlook. Bass also found the Japanese managers to be older, with a slower rate of advancement than managers in the United States, Britain, The Netherlands, Belgium, Germany, Austria, Latin America, and India. The Japanese sample rated high on empathy and risk-taking and were more willing to spend money on product quality. They did not value prestige, security, or pleasure as highly as managers from the other countries, however. The sample also appeared to want cooperation with their peers and were more willing to discuss their feelings with others as well as to tolerate conflict. Their life goals were more apt to include self-realization, leadership, expertness, independence, and duty.

Achievement Orientation

McClelland and Winter (1969) suggested that a society's orientation toward work and achievement is the major determinant of economic performance. McClelland et al. (1953) described achievers as moderate risk takers who thrive on innovation and novel situations, are future oriented, and obtain satisfaction from immediate feedback that indicates that they have obtained success as a result of their own efforts. Furthermore, McClelland (1962) pointed to achievement motivation as the direct cause of the economic rise and fall of nations. Atkinson (1977), Atkinson and Feather (1966), and Atkinson and Raynor (1974) have verified the impact of the achievement motive on individual, organizational, and national business success.

To illustrate:

- In cameras, at least half a dozen major companies vigorously compete for shares of the domestic market.
- In color televisions, industry leaders must be content with closer runner-ups.
- In hi-fi equipment, Technics and Pioneer slug it out with Sansui, Sony, and many others.
- In automobiles, Toyota and Nissan strive for the first place position of Mitsubishi. Toyo Kogyo (Mazda), and others nip at their heels. (Heenan 1983, p. 43)

Adaptation

Adaptation is the ability to copy and modify original concepts: product ideas, management concepts, or technical know-how. Japan has extensively borrowed several manufacturing and management ideas from the West, as its investment in pure and basic research is not comparable to Western levels. Although this is true to a large extent, in recent years, Japan has turned to more basic research in selected growth areas such as information systems and sophisticated communications equipment.

In marketing its products, Japan has outperformed the United States through meticulous adaptation of "the marketing concept," that is, a company philosophy that emphasizes customer orientation as the focal point for a firm's survival and growth. This is well demonstrated by the Japanese automobile makers in their ability to capture a significant market share in the American and European markets very quickly. Japan, as a neophyte, holds 30 percent of all small car sales in the United States and thus poses a serious threat to the American automobile industry. Japan has also skillfully adapted many other marketing ideas, including segmentation, product positioning, product life cycle theory, and new product development strategies.

In whatever ideas they have copied, the Japanese have been innovative in their adaptation. Therefore, Japan deserves to be called "innovative-adapted." Surprisingly, it has managed to adapt Western production and marketing techniques without disturbing its basic socioeconomic fabric. That is why "the Japanese society," says Prime Minister Lee Kuan Yew of Singapore, "is an illustration in Darwinian evolution, the survival of the most resilient social organization" (Heenan 1983, p. 43).

GOVERNMENT: SERVING THE BUSINESS SECTOR

Many scholars suggest that the success of Japan is largely attributable to strong bonds and collaboration between Japanese government and business firms (Heenan 1983, p. 122; Vogel 1978, p. 161). In Japan, government bureaucrats take it as their serious mission to direct, control, and supervise various economic activities and policies to achieve economic success for the nation. The government aids industry in many forms. For instance, the government arranges low-interest financing and guarantees from a variety of quasi-governmental agencies, helps in forming corporate consortia, assures domestic markets, and insures against foreign exchange risks (Heenan 1983, p. 41).

Industrial capital in Japan normally comes from the banks rather than from external capital markets. Since the banks obtain their loan money from the government, the latter may exert considerable pressure on the banks whenever necessary. Therefore, unlike American managers, the Japanese managers are not too concerned about shareholders, and thus they are willing to take greater risks.

Some of the key government and quasi-governmental agencies are: the Ministry of Finance (MOF), the Ministry of International Trade and Industry (MITI), the prime minister's office, the Cabinet, the Diet, and Keidanren (the Federation of Economic Organizations). Government officials in these agencies consider it one of their basic missions to guide and encourage industries that they expect to become increasingly competitive internationally (these are known as "sunrise" industries). Conversely, they discourage industries that seem unlikely to remain competitive ("sunset" industries). To companies in promising industries, the government grants choice locations of reclaimed land and permission to expand and build new plants. The government creates tax advantages for companies that modernize their plants and raises licensing standards to force companies to modernize.

In international trade, government officials encourage and help companies with surplus capital in making foreign investment decisions, establishing insurance systems to provide security for such investments, and negotiating international trade agreements that help rising Japanese industries.

JAPANESE BUSINESS: SPIRITUAL GOALS DOMINATE OVER PROFIT GOALS

Japanese business aspirations tend to lean somewhat toward spiritual rather than materialistic goals such as profit. True, profits are required for the survival of a business, but they do not substitute for nonmaterialistic goals such as perpetual maintenance of "harmony" among all parties and peoples. The basis for such Japanese business values and work ethic is the Zen spirit (to be selfless) (Takeuchi 1982, p. 8), and Confucian values that underpin their culture and tradition. These, in turn, influence Japanese organizational structures and management systems. Great importance is given to collectivity: the supremacy of the group's rights and goals over the individual's. The individual's needs are subservient to those of the group. Deviators from this are punished through social shame or ostracism, which is feared by people more than death in close societies like Japan.

Thus, Japanese business philosophy emphasizes national and company long-term goals more than short-term profits. Against this background, the distinct features of the Japanese managerial systems are: lifetime employment; a seniority-based reward system; and a heavy involvement of management in the lives of the workers, what is known as "industrial paternalism."

Also, the Japanese have a different "Total Quality" concept, the scope of which is much broader than in the United States. Moreover, quality and productivity are regarded as inseparable. Combined with product quality and productivity, the quality of working life forms the foundation of "sound business practices." By comparison, Americans, for instance, regard products or things from the perspective of the Judeo-Christian ethic that things exist for the use of human beings. However, the Japanese perceive products as having their own spirits that need to be respected and cared for.

LABOR: HARMONIOUS RELATIONSHIP WITH MANAGEMENT

Labor unions began in Japan with the American occupation of the country after World War II. Although Japan has its share of costly labor strikes, the important point is the harmonious relationship between management and union.

Generally, workers develop a high sense of identity with their firms that is partly due to modest differences between management and workers; workers have no rich capitalist class above them whose lifestyle is dramatically different from theirs. The cooperativeness of unions is best seen in the care of their unquestioned acceptance of modern innovations and decisions of Japanese industries to relocate manufacturing plants abroad, even though these actions threaten domestic employment. Since many Japanese firms have profit-sharing methods, the workers get their part of the benefits. Consequently, the Japanese workers believe in innovations and even their firms' compliance with foreign pressures, as long as these actions help their firms to make more profits.

PUBLIC: THE LOYAL CITIZENS

The Japanese public has a high sense of loyalty to its nation and will make any sacrifice necessary to put its nation in the front. As stated earlier, because of their unique historic, socioeconomic, and cultural background, being united to work for a common purpose has become a necessary survival strategy for the Japanese people.

In addition, government, business, and various social organizations continually perpetuate patriotism and cultural heritage and values through propaganda, patriotic songs in factories, and so on. As an example of how the government perpetuates patriotism, a government communication to the public reads as follows:

Loyalty to the State requires citizens to show love for it in the right way. Indifference to the existence of one's own nation, and disregard for its values amounts to a hatred of one's own nation. (Pascale and Athos 1981, p. 189)

Other admirable characteristics of the Japanese people are their frugal nature, patience, persistence, diligence, and ability to quickly acquire new skills and adapt them to changing circumstances.

"EXPORT-PUSH" FACTORS: THE ENVIRONMENTAL FACTOR

The "export-push" factors are Japanese actions and tactics that have been major catalytic agents in the country's export growth. These factors do not include events or conditions outside Japan that may have stimulated demand for Japanese products. The major export-push factors are:

- To build exports through market share objectives;
- To price their product competitively;
- To provide share objectives and terms and conditions to middlemen;
- To be competitive in product designs.

The Japanese have been known to introduce their products at competitively low prices initially and thereby influence a gradual increase in market share. For example, in introducing Japanese automobiles into the United States, the Japanese have had to wait until an appropriate time (the oil crisis in the mid-1970s) to gain a substantial market share for their products. They have been very skillful in using (and still continue to use) the American marketing concepts and techniques, "the marketing concept," product design, product positioning, and pricing strategies, for example.

Among other factors, pricing and liberal financing terms to dealers and customers have become important tools. If Japanese firms perceive a threat to their present or future market position, they quickly retaliate by updating or redesigning their product line and thereby keep a step ahead of their former and would-be challenger(s). This is evident in their present aggressive push in microcomputers.

"IMPORT-PULL" FACTORS: AN EXTERNAL ENVIRONMENTAL FACTOR

The "import-pull" factors play an equally significant role in the Japanese economic miracle. These are internal considerations of other nations that produce a conducive environment for Japan to export its products. For instance, in the United States, the following conditions have been found to be beneficial for the Japanese exports:

• Changes within the U.S. competitive environment;

• Changes in consumer attitudes;

• Policy decisions or actions by U.S. firms and government;

• Positions taken by U.S. labor that have afforded Japanese producers a better opportunity to gain and hold increased market shares. (Monroe 1978, p. 192)

The changes within the U.S. competitive environment have come about since World War II when the U.S. government began Keynesian economic measures to boost "aggregate demand." Maintaining full employment through increased government spending in order to build aggregate demand became a national objective. With more governmental intervention in the economy, free enterprise and competitive systems have found more and more regulations curbing the freedom of the American firms.

Modern consumers are more knowledgeable about various products and markets. With government trying to maintain a full employment policy and easy credit availability compared with other nations, American consumers tend to indulge in excessive consumption, thus providing vast markets for a variety of products. Product quality and price are the main consumer considerations rather than whether the product is "Made in the U.S.A." or elsewhere.

Another import-pull factor was caused by the ever-declining quality of American-made products relative to those from Japan. The decline in quality and workmanship has been attributed to changing values in American life, from hard work to an easy life and saving to spending.

Also, it was alleged that the American worker, over time through union bargaining, became the world's highest paid laborer without a corresponding contribution to an increase in productivity. In addition, there have been many costly labor strikes in the United States compared with Japan, adding to the costs of production and thus making American products noncompetitive in price or quality with the Japanese products.

On the other hand, pressured by demanding shareholders who would always prefer to have their periodic dividends regularly, American management has been in constant pursuit of short-term profits rather than the long-range survival strategies, thus negatively affecting the ability of American firms to compete in international markets and even in domestic markets.

Finally, government's polices in the form of inducement to stimulate new investment or modernize the existing production pattern have tended to be either too slow or have not come at all in certain major industries. Ironically, however, the government has provided a growing number of welfare programs to meet certain socioeconomic objectives, hoping to buttress aggregate demand. Although the Reagan administration attempted to reverse these trends to some extent, the effects of past governmental actions still pervade and still provide conducive factors for import-pull.

To summarize, in reality, the export-push and import-pull factors work in unison. Their combined effect can be compared to the actions of the blades of a pair of scissors. Which blade is more important at a point in time can hardly be determined (Monroe 1978, p. 206).

SUMMARY OF THE MODEL

The Japanese have been able to achieve their "economic miracle" not by sheer accident or by luck, but by careful planning and missionary zeal in setting certain economic goals and achieving them. No doubt this achievement wouldn't have been possible without the benevolent support of the Japanese government, which played a key role in planning, goal setting, coordinating, and sometimes financially supporting various business ventures that were important to Japanese economic progress. Also, the Japanese government has been responsible for molding and/ or modifying behaviors of the general public, labor, and other concerned bodies accordingly. Thus, in the ultimate analysis, it was the interaction of three major behavioral variables, namely, attitude, achievement orientation, and adaptability of the Japanese that made the Japan economic miracle possible. The hardworking Japanese were fortunate to have favorable external circumstances such as the worldwide import-pull factors, particularly from the market-rich; and internal export-push factors, a historical necessity for a land-locked, natural-resource-poor country. A combination of the above factors created a synergistic effect that was responsible for the enormous economic success of Japan, much beyond its expectations. The espoused model may not be directly applicable to other countries, especially if they have a drastically different socioeconomic heritage. Nevertheless, the model can be an "eye-opener" for other nations to examine the Japanese success and a caution for them not to emulate the Japanese blindly without understanding their particular and peculiar circumstances. Finally, the process of technology transfer needs to be carefully monitored by both donor and host country to see that a given technology is properly assimilated and put to maximum use. The host country should take the initiative in formulating appropriate strategies for this process to take place.

CONCLUSION

To conclude, technology transfer, to be successful, should be carefully monitored by the DCs as well as the LDCs. In-depth analytical study must be made before acquiring new technologies. Once acquired, an all-out effort must be made to adapt the new technology to the unique environment of the recipient country. The donor nations not only get the price for the technology they transfer, they also get some feedback in terms of reverse engineering that can be built into the agreement. Finally, LDCs can become new markets for DC products like airplanes, telecommunications equipment, agricultural machinery, earthmoving equipment, fertilizers, and so on. Thus, technology transfer can be seen as mutually beneficial to both donor and recipient countries.

Chapter Six

Application of the Model: India

This chapter presents the case of India, an example of how technology transfer could be successful. If India and other developing countries were to follow the example of Japan and other successful countries in the Pacific Basin, rapid economic growth could be within their reach. However, success depends not only on analyzing others' economic successes but also on willingness to undergo necessary sacrifices to achieve the growth (Reddy and Campbell 1994). It calls for more than emulation. As stated in Chapter 5, the assimilation of the technology into the economic system of a country is vital. This chapter presents a new macro-behavioral economic growth model. It is different from the traditional economic models that generally consider growth as a result of the right mix of land, labor, capital, and entrepreneurship (Campbell and Brue 1990). On the other hand, the macro-behavioral economic model assumes that economic growth can be achieved by nurturing appropriate behavioral characteristics in a nation's population.

The adaptiveness, achievement orientation, and attitudes of the Japanese people have been identified as critical to Japan's economic success (see Figure 6.1 later in this chapter). Additionally, Japan was aided by factors such as total support from the government and a cooperative spirit between industry and labor unions. These features are further helped by the nationalistic attitude of the Japanese, who prefer Japanese-made products to imports. Finally, Japan also took advantage of the import-pull factors prevailing in the Western markets. By coupling this with its own aggressive export-push strategy, Japan had quickly established beachheads into lucrative Western markets. To date, it continues to hold and build market shares in these countries. The Japanese exports continue unabated, undaunted by competition and host governments' pressures. The Japanese businesses have learned to outperform their competitors and neutralize the hostile governments continually by establishing joint ventures in those nations. The purpose of this chapter is to present issues relating to application of the macro-behavioral economic development model to India. India is chosen as an example because it has all, if not most, of the diverse characteristics of a typical developing country in the free world.

BACKGROUND

India's economy is a mixture of traditional village farming and handicrafts, modern agriculture, old and new branches of industry, and a multitude of support services. It presents both the entrepreneurial skills and drives of the capitalist system and widespread government intervention of the socialist mold (Cateora 1993). Growth of 4 percent to 5 percent annually in the 1990s has softened the impact of population growth on unemployment, social tranquility, and the environment. Agricultural output has continued to expand, reflecting the greater use of modern farming techniques and improved seed that have helped to make India self-sufficient in food grains and a net agricultural exporter. However, tens of millions of villagers, particularly in the South, have not benefited from the Green Revolution, and live in abject poverty. Industry has benefited from a partial liberalization of controls. The growth rate of the service sector is often subject to lower foreign exchange reserves, higher inflation, and a large debt service burden. The inflation rate was 10 percent in 1992.

In 1990, India's GNP was $254 billion and the per capita income reached $300; national income was $34 billion; and national expenditure reached $54 billion. Due to high expenses involved in purchasing oil, capital goods, technology, and servicing the cost of foreign debt, India has been consistently incurring annual budget deficits for the last two decades. These deficits are expected to continue until the country can eliminate them through export earnings and reduce import expenses simultaneously.

India's major crops include rice, cereals, pulses, oilseed, cotton, and others. The country has abundant coal—the fourth largest reserves in the world—and minerals like iron ore, manganese, mica, and bauxite. India's major industries are textiles, food processing, and steel. In 1985, the labor force consisted of 284.4 million; the unemployment rate exceeded 10 percent. In 1990, India's exports totaled $17 billion, and consisted of gems and jewelry, engineering goods, clothing, textiles, chemicals, tea, coffee, and fish products. Major trading partners are the European Community (25 percent), the United States (19 percent), the former Soviet Union and

Eastern Europe (17 percent), and Japan (10 percent). Imports totaled about $25 billion consisting of petroleum, capital goods, uncut gems and jewelry, chemicals, iron and steel, and edible oils, representing the following countries/regions: the European Community (33 percent), the Middle East (19 percent), Japan (10 percent), the United States (9 percent), and the former Soviet Union and Eastern Europe (8 percent).

India is a member of major international organizations such as GATT, IBRD, ILO, IMO, IFC, and others. Its annual industrial production growth rate was 5 percent. The major industries include textiles, food processing, steel, machinery, transportation equipment, cement, jute manufacture, mining, petroleum, power, chemicals, pharmaceuticals, and electronics. Agriculture accounts for about 30 percent of GNP and employs 67 percent of labor force. Principal crops include rice, wheat, oilseed, cotton, jute, tea, sugar cane, and potatoes. It has substantial livestock that includes cattle, buffalo, sheep, goats, and poultry. Fish catch is about three million metric tons, which places India among the world's top ten fishing nations.

India maintains a watchful, but generally peaceful, relationship with two unfriendly neighbors, Pakistan and China, and continues to play a leading role in the nonaligned movement. The Green Revolution of the 1970s has made the country self-sufficient in food production for the first time since the nineteenth century. The country has a large, well-educated middle class and a growing industrial economy. During 1992 the Rao government attempted to foster economic growth by relaxing the centralized planning controls on international trade and investment that had long stifled the nation's potential.

Nevertheless, the nation faces persistent problems, including separatist movements, regional grievances, and communal conflicts. Much of the population (65 percent) consists of illiterate people living in rural and urban poverty or near-poverty; the benefits of modernization have been unevenly distributed. Corruption is rife in politics and business. Measures to control population growth have been generally unsuccessful. India's historical legacy of diversity and disunity continues to complicate the country's transformation into a modern state.

To reverse the above trend, India has embarked on new programs for liberalizing the economy and abandoning the elaborate protectionist controls and state monopolies. Foreign investment is being wooed. Public enterprises are being abandoned except defense, mining and petroleum, and railways. These friendly overtures to foreign investors have led to a rush of proposals of investment from such firms as IBM, GM, GE, Coca-Cola, and McDonald's. Cateora (1993) hopes that India will somehow expand its investment horizons and become part of the economic development boom that until now has passed it by. The country has the potential to become a more prosperous nation, provided proper actions are quickly taken.

WEAKNESSES

Major problems continue to slow India's plans and dreams for economic growth. Although some of these detractors can be eliminated, some over a period of time, the rest probably will continue for a long time. Nevertheless, these limiting weaknesses can at least be reduced, if not removed. The most important problems troubling Indian economic growth can be categorized as follows:

1. The infrastructure
2. Corruption
3. Overpopulation
4. Religious conflicts
5. Education
6. Government-owned industries
7. Poverty
8. The lack of export drive

The Infrastructure

India's present infrastructure is largely a by-product of what the British regime had set up to administer the country and move military troops to maintain law and order. Its railroads, seaports, airports, and roads were developed with the same objective. Since independence, though the country has been adding to that base, significant highway systems, railroads, and waterways need to be further developed to help accelerate economic growth. In addition, banking, insurance, and various other business services industries must be rapidly established and maintained. Developing the country without first developing proper infrastructure will only paralyze the existing meager infrastructure. Therefore, planners should emphasize extensive development of roads, railroads, seaports, airports, canal ways, and so on. These improvements will help speed up the development process.

According to Ramaswamy and Namakumari (1990, pp. 47–49), India has a large infrastructure sector consisting of coal, petroleum, power, the transport system, the banking system, and so on, registering a good growth of 10 percent per year over the past decade.

In coal, India produces 85 percent of its energy requirements and it has increased its oil reserves since 1975. Still, imports contribute nearly half its requirements each year. In power, India is the tenth largest producer of power in the world. Although this sector has undergone a high degree of technological sophistication, still the power capacity of the country is very inadequate.

India's railway system is the largest in Asia and the fourth largest in the world. Originating freight traffic has gone up from 44 billion ton km to 183 billion ton km. Originating passenger traffic has risen from 67 billion passenger km to 229 billion passenger km. The road transport has increased; the number of trucks on the road has increased from 82,000 to more than 7.6 lakhs. An extensive network of feeder routes has been developed. The rural road network has crossed the six-lakh mark. Yet, the quality of the roads must improve greatly so that they can be used even during the heavy monsoons.

Port facilities in India have grown substantially; traffic handled by Indian ports went up from 19 million tons to 107 million tons. The number of major ports went up from five to ten.

Air traffic in 1950–1951 was practically negligible. By 1984–1985, air traffic had gone up to 664 million ton km. Indian Airlines today is the second largest domestic air carrier in the world outside the United States. There are five international airports and 85 other airdromes in the country. Air India, the international airline of India, is one of the middle-ranking international airlines.

India's banking system has registered significant growth. At the end of 1984, there were 255 scheduled commercial banks, 28 of them real giants. The number of rural branches rose from 1,832 in 1969 to 27,411 in 1984.

India has a well-established post and telegraph system owned and operated by the central government. In addition, in the last few years, the introduction of fax machines and so on into the country has enhanced the communications facilities in the country to some extent, but India has still a long way to go to match its communications infrastructure to those of the neighboring Singapore, Malaysia, and other faster-developing countries. Today, there are various satellite television channels available, including CNN from Atlanta.

Corruption

Corruption is widespread in the country. It is like a cancer that destroys the social, moral, and entrepreneurial spirit in a society. In India, as in most other developing countries, corruption is present in all walks of life. Corruption in government and business has become a way of life, as it has in Brazil or Mexico. Unless people, government, and business jointly work to eradicate or neutralize corruption, achieving rapid economic growth will not be easy.

Overpopulation

Overpopulation is another major problem. Eighty percent of the population lives in villages and a great majority of them are poor. The poor are multiplying fast, as they feel having many male children is a form of security in their old age. This is one basic reason why India's family planning programs have been repeatedly crippled; it is due to the lack of public support. Unlike China, where population growth is strictly controlled by its communist government, the democratic form of government in India is not able to carry out programs that are unpopular with the people. The government should continue relentlessly educating its citizens regarding the disadvantages of the overpopulation and encourage birth control simultaneously.

Religious Conflicts

India is a home of many religious groups—Hindus, Moslems, Christians, and others. Often, the religious differences can easily be exploited by unscrupulous politicians for their own ends. Ambitious politicians try to exploit religious differences in a country for their own benefit. Unless people are alerted to this, and preemptive measures are taken by the government, religious and ethnic conflicts will continue to disrupt the economic progress of the nation. Instability caused by ethnic conflict discourages necessary foreign investment.

Education

Knowledge is power. To possess knowledge, a nation's population must be able to read and write and understand the democratic process. India has come a long way, since its independence in 1947, to enhance the literacy rate in the country. Today's literacy rate is about 40 percent. When compared to countries like Japan, where it is 100 percent, or even China, where the literacy rate is much higher than that of India, India needs to do more work on this front. Compulsory elementary education for all children must be rigorously carried out. Adult education programs must also be vigorously pursued throughout the nation.

Government-Owned Industries

In India, government is a major industrial power. Major industries like iron, steel, and transport are often government-owned. Initially, state ownership was thought of as a process to provide capital and employment to eliminate concentration of wealth in a few hands. However, the state-owned and -operated enterprises, with a few exceptions, have turned out to be less efficient than privately-owned businesses, because employees have no motivation to produce profits, since jobs are almost permanent. To reverse the trend, recently the government has begun to privatize industries that were until now out of reach to private and foreign investors.

Poverty

There is no bigger obstacle to achieving economic growth than poverty. Poor people who live a hand-to-mouth existence will be least concerned about how best they can contribute to the nation's economic growth. Therefore, eradicating poverty must be the sincere goal for India's politicians, not simply a platform to serve their ends. Unless people are provided with opportunities to pursue occupations and businesses through low-interest loans and free training facilities, the country's poverty cannot be eradicated. The published unemployment rate is about 20 percent, but real unemployment could be higher than that.

The Lack of Export Drive

India has traditionally been an exporter of raw materials and an importer of finished goods. Since becoming independent from Britain in 1947, India has been gradually building its industrial might. Today it is self-sufficient in most basic goods, some luxury goods like cosmetics, basic pharmaceuticals, and so on, but it continues to import capital goods, aircraft, computers, and the like. Most important, oil imports keep draining its precious foreign exchange reserves. Table 6.1 shows that India is moving toward becoming a major exporter. The process is slow. India had a positive balance of trade of $8 billion in 1988–1989; however, it had a balance of trade deficits in each of the other years since 1990. Foreign currency reserves have increased to $20 billion in 1992–1993 due to major foreign investments into the country.

THE MODEL

As shown in Figure 6.1, a positive attitude toward achieving economic growth through domestic and foreign private investment and aggressive export orientation is central to India's economic prosperity. Since its independence, India has vacillated in choosing between private and public, and domestic and foreign investment. Fear of exploitation by private and foreign businesses has always been the guiding philosophy behind the formulation of the country's economic development plans. However, with new export promotion programs and facilities established by the

Table 6.1
India's Foreign Trade, 1983–1993 (in Crores of Rupees) [1 Crore = 10,000,00; and U.S. $1 = Rs. 32 approx. in 1992]

Year	Imports	Exports	Balance of Trade	%Financed by Exports	Foreign Currency Reserves
1983–84	15,763	9,872	−5,891	63	5,498
1984–85	17,092	11,555	−5,537	68	6,817
1985–86	19,658	10,895	−8,763	55	7,384
1986–87	20,084	12,567	−7,517	63	7,645
1987–88	22,343	15,719	−6,624	70	7,282
1988–89	28,235	20,332	8,004	72	6,605
1989–90	35,412	27,681	−7,731	78	5,787
1990–91	43,198	32,553	10,645	75	4,388
1991–92	47,851	44,041	−3,810	92	14,578
1992–93	63,378	53,688	−9,687	85	20,141

Source: R. L. Varshney and B. Bhattacharyya, *International Marketing: An Indian Perspective*, 8th ed. (New Delhi, India: Sultan Chand and Sons, 1994), p. 92.

government, India's export marketing is expected to become more competitive in the future.

Import-pull factors in the West and the United States following World War II have greatly helped Japan to build up its industrial machine. Capitalizing on the favorable situation for imports, Japan has quickly become a mass producer and exporter of quality goods at competitive prices and an expert at effectively marketing its goods to the United States and Western countries. Japan's friendly relations with the United States have always been a great asset in this regard.

Although India did not share the same friendly relations with the United States and the West, due to its fixation with nonaligned countries, it could use the same nonaligned countries' markets to export its goods. Nevertheless, it cannot neglect the markets of the rich EC, United States, and Japan, and the newly emerging markets in the former Soviet Union and Eastern Europe. These markets must be quickly cultivated and maintained through exporting high-quality products at competitive prices. Also, Indian businesses must improve the quality of their marketing,

Figure 6.1
Integrated Macro-Behavioral Model

Import-Pull Factors

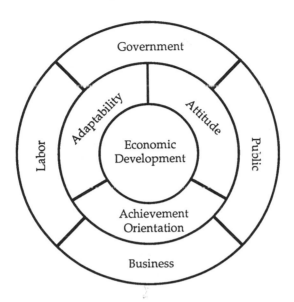

Export-Push Factors

Source: Adapted from Allan C. Reddy, John E. Oliver, C. P. Rao, and A. L. Addington, "A Macro-Behavioral Model of the Japanese Economic Miracle," *Akron Business and Economic Review* (Spring 1984), p. 41.

particularly by improving their product, distribution, promotion, and price competitiveness. The negative image that Indian goods often carry among importers, for lack of consistent product quality and timely delivery, must be erased through better business practices.

India can hasten its economic growth by adapting the economic development model that worked well for Japan and to its NIC Asian neighbors. India needs stability as a matter of law and order. Also, there is a tremendous need for stable policies that can be established and carried out. A generalized administration suited to colonial rule must be replaced by professionalism. More developing countries have to realize that there is greater need for regional cooperation, because the leverage they had with the rich and powerful nations has significantly decreased with the ending of the Cold War. Unfortunately, the South Asian planners have yet to accept this.

Besides regional cooperation with its surrounding neighbors, gulf countries, and Southeast Asian nations including Japan, India must not ignore the prospects of doing business with China and Russia more aggressively. Economic complementarity does exist between India and Russia and can be expanded, as is happening between China and Russia. India's interests will be well served by developing all Asian linkages, including Japan.

The need for reform and liberalization, and becoming a player in the global marketplace has been largely accepted as essential for development of the Indian economy. Indian history, like that of any other country, has its cycle of glory and weaknesses. India needs no lessons on human rights and civil liberties. It needs only to live up to the codes laid down by culture and tradition requiring self-discipline and self-regulation, and a commitment to the community and nation.

IMPLICATIONS

India and other developing economies can succeed in their economic growth plans by using models that have been successful in other countries, especially Japan and the Pacific Basin NICs. Often, India's planners and other important people get caught up in rhetoric and ignore the importance of behavioral characteristics necessary to promote rapid economic growth in a nation. It is the responsibility of the country's leaders, politicians, planners, bureaucrats, and educators to plant and nurture the right attitudes, aspirations, and adaptive-mindedness among the people. This can be done through media, films, seminars, television programs, and so on. Also, it is important to remember that economic growth cannot be achieved without other countries' help, especially the rich and developed countries. Therefore, relationships with these countries are important and friendly relationships must be maintained with these nations before asking their help. The Japanese could not possibly achieve economic development without cultivating friendly relationships with the United States and the West. Ironically, Japan fought a major war with the United States. Therefore, India also needs to look for cooperation from other countries and seek synergies. It is rather sad that although the country is blessed with enormous intellectual capital, it is unable to realize its economic dreams because of neglect of the role played by behavioral characteristics in economic development.

AN OPTIMISTIC LOOK AT INDIA, USING THE INTEGRATED MACRO-BEHAVIORAL MODEL

While there continue to be barriers to growth, as described earlier in this chapter, there is also reason for considerable optimism. This section draws on analysis ("Two Asian Giants, Growing Apart") done by Karen

Elliot House, president of the International Group of Dow Jones, re-ported in a recent edition of the *Wall Street Journal* (February 24, 1995), and applies it to the Integrated Macro-Behavioral Model developed by Reddy et al. (1994). A closer look at the people of India reveals that, even in socialism and religious strife, two possible barriers to growth, there is reason for optimism. India is gradually shifting away from self-imposed shackles of socialism toward capitalism without rejecting its rich and diverse culture.

Like the United States, India is a melting pot of peoples, religions, and territories held together by free will, expressed by voters at the ballot box. Thus, religious riots in Bombay between Muslims and Hindus and other periodic disturbances among different religious groups in the country do not show a crumbling of Indian socioeconomic and political structure any more than riots in Los Angeles foreshadow the fall of American democracy.

Business

In today's India, business is going through an incredible surge. Indians have traditionally proved themselves to be as good businesspersons as the Chinese. Just as Chinese have shown their business mettle by creating thriving restaurant businesses globally, Indians have expanded into mo-tel businesses, especially in the United States, Canada, and the United Kingdom. Perhaps Indians understand profits better than Chinese, as they are willing to maintain win-win relationships in doing business with Westerners. India today has a large and long-established private sector and has the more active stock exchange, in the business center of Bombay. Foreign investors can choose among Indian partners or invest-ments with established business history.

Labor

If we define labor as the sum of the workforce, India has many of the right ingredients. India is a rich source for employees in engineering, medicine, education, and computer software. Additionally, because of the three hundred-year British rule in the past and English influences in many aspects of Indian life, Indians have less difficulty in coping with cultures where English is the primary language.

Government

Though corruption is endemic in India, as it is in China, it is an open topic of critical discussion in the press these days, in parliament and among businessmen themselves. Therefore, smart American investors are beginning to look at India as a land of opportunity with an enormous population base. With close to one billion in numbers, India is the second largest in population in the world, following China. Most important, there is a new middle class that is emerging rapidly. The market size of this new middle class consists of some 200 million people, and such a market cannot simply be ignored by many growth-conscious multinational firms. Furthermore, on the surface, India might appear unstable, but it is quite stable inside. In contrast, China may appear to be quite stable from outside, but not so stable from within.

Attitude, Achievement Orientation, and Adaptability

India is going through a marketing and business revolution with a passion that is comparable to a religious revival. Comments and opinions by Westerners in general reflect a growing trend of favorable attitudes, achievement orientation, and adaptability—consistent with the postulated behavioral growth model in this book.

Economic Development

India, like China, still has a long way to go to become a fully hospitable environment for business and investment. India's economic growth lags behind China's; its gross national product is expected to grow by 5.5 percent in 1994, less than half China's anticipated 12 percent annual rate. And population in India is growing at 2 percent a year—well above China, where stringent birth control programs have almost stabilized population.

SUMMARY

Analyses of prevailing trends in India and opinions of authorities on the business climate in India leave considerable room for a positive outlook. The Integrated Macro-Behavioral Model can continue to be used to identify the strengths and the areas needing improvement. Already signs are evident that India is picking up speed in its economic developments. Some countries like the Netherlands now no longer consider India a low-income country, but a middle-income country, and therefore no longer needing economic aid from developed countries. India is rapidly becoming an international player in high technology. Electronics production reached $4.4 billion in 1988, and the industry is expected to grow about 30 percent annually for the rest of the century (Rayner 1989). To sustain the economic growth that it has achieved in recent years and to develop the country further in a balanced manner, India needs to follow closely the qualitative growth model suggested in this chapter.

Conclusions

The major purpose of this book has been to study the process of technology transfer to developing countries and to suggest strategies that would benefit both donor and host countries. The dynamics of the modern world are such that unless technology transfers are carefully planned and carried out, the expected economic development in the LDCs might not take place and efforts to transfer technology are thus wasted. Regulation of transfers is difficult because of lack of recording procedures. Besides, for many reasons, firms that transfer technology may not like to report the transfers. They may like to maintain confidentiality. Also, there may not be any reports on technology transfers that fail in their early stages. Neither the donor nor the recipient report about such incidences, due to embarrassment. In the absence of a mechanism to regulate the transfers, at least, the participants need to be more cognizant of both positive and negative aspects of the transfer process.

We have made several assumptions regarding the benefits of the technology transfer: Countries would ask and get the correct types of technologies, and donor countries would assess the needs of the host countries correctly and give them appropriate technologies. Improper technologies or improper transfers of technologies are improvident. In either case, the host country will abandon the transferred technology eventually because of the lack of a correct "fit."

The prognosis for future technology transfers appears mixed, and perhaps it will remain so for a long time to come. On the one hand, there is optimism that advanced nations would be willing to transfer consumer and industrial goods and services technologies in their own profit-making interests. On the other hand, for fear of creating competition for their own manufactured goods, advanced nations may not be forthcoming to share most recent technologies as compared to older or obsolete technologies. Thus, for example, they would be more willing to give away a ten-year-old automobile manufacturing technology than the more recent type.

It appears that the LDCs have limited choices—whether they take whatever technology they can get or live without it. But, the argument in this book is about the technology assimilation process. That is, once a technology is obtained, it should be put to maximum use. The developing countries have a big gap to fill in economic development. Therefore, the LDCs should carefully evaluate a technology and its applicability to the individual circumstances of the country before they embrace it. Here again, what is a successful technology in one LDC may not be the same in another because of the socioeconomic, cultural, religious, and other differences among the LDCs.

In Chapter 1, we discussed the definitions and analyzed the entire process of technology transfer. That technology transfer is limited to consumer and industrial goods manufacturing and marketing is also explained. In Chapter 2, we presented the major players in technology transfer within a developed country like the United States. In Chapter 3, we discussed the barriers and solutions to the transfer from the DCs to the LDCs. There are more problems than solutions here. Therefore, careful adaptation of new technologies is necessary. The LDCs cannot afford to waste their resources carelessly on technologies that might not work for them. Chapter 4 dealt with the ethical issues involved in the transfer process. The DCs have many reservations in transferring technologies, one of them being whether or not a country is violating human rights. We discussed the technology transfer assimilation model in Chapter 5 and extended its application to a large LDC—India—in Chapter 6. The model presents a novel concept that focuses around the behavioral characteristics of the population as important to receive, absorb, and make use of new technologies that are transferred to them from advanced nations. The model is extended to an LDC like India. India has benefited a great deal from imported technology, but by comparison to its Asian neighbors like Singapore, Hong Kong, South Korea, Taiwan, and others, it lags behind in adapting and assimilating technologies to foster its economic growth.

Additional viewpoints relating to technology transfer are included in the appendices. Professor Ira Saltz argues about the negative effects of technology transfer. Jerry Ladman describes the process of technology transfer from a broader and an earlier perspective in that he covers points that are included in the current introductory chapter. Finally, we added an untested model, the reciprocal distribution (RD) paradigm, as a way to transfer technology from developed to developing countries.

The developed countries will have more to benefit from the RD arrangement than the developing countries.

IMPLICATIONS

In concluding, the following points need to be remembered:

1. Technology transfers when properly done provide big benefits to both donor and recipient countries. The recipient countries prosper economically and the donor nations will find new markets for their products.
2. Technology transfer should be carefully monitored and regulated through an autonomous body representing the members of both developed and developing countries. Though the function of the body is advisory, this organization should be a reservoir of information regarding the donors, recipients, technologies, and the success or failure of the transfers by date and country, and so on.
3. Developing countries cannot simply rely on donor countries to find and transfer proper technologies. Instead, they should also develop their own research and development organization to investigate and find out what would be appropriate technologies for them. This process will help the LDCs in their developmental process. Also, the LDCs should be prepared to pay the right price to attract donor countries for technologies that they are willing to transfer. For instance, through a certain procedure, human waste and garbage can be converted into electrical energy. This cheap source of bio-gas-produced energy is a boon for many LDCs that are burdened with overpopulation and meager resources.
4. The ethical aspects and human side effects related to technology transfer cannot be neglected. A thorough study of these issues must be made before, during, and after a transfer is made.

In the final analysis, the goals of host and donor nations are different. The donors would like to maximize return on investments by donor countries, and the recipients would like to receive appropriate technologies at the lowest cost possible. Home countries will continue to control technology transfers for national security and for tax revenues. It is unlikely that controls to protect international competitiveness will be developed. Leaders among developed nations are even becoming more cautious about giving technology away freely.

Third World nations must follow a framework in evaluating technologies that are viable. There are no magic solutions to the transfer problem. However, following a systematic path to solve the problem would immensely help a totally bewildering set of scenarios. The following approach (Table 7.1) is suggested by Alkhafaji (1995, pp. 266–269).

The framework, as summarized in Table 7.1, is exploratory and is designed to clarify the important stages of technology transfer and to serve

Table 7.1
Strategic Framework for Acquiring New Technology

Stage	Requirements
1. Preidentification	Determine national goals (i.e., develop the agricultural or industrial sector or accommodate social needs)
2. Identification	Assess managerial capabilities and identify the necessary infrastructure
3. Alternatives	Look at other sources and determine a fair price
4. Evaluation	Evaluate the alternatives and determine the best form of investment (i.e., licensing, joint venture, or wholly owned)
5. Selection	Select the most appropriate choice
6. Implementation	Determine specifications, programs, policies, timetables, resources, changes to the organizational structure, and reward and performance evaluation systems

as a tool for LDCs in acquiring new technology. The framework includes four major steps that must be followed before any decision to acquire new technology takes place, plus guidelines for selection and implementation.

PREIDENTIFICATION STAGE

The first stage precedes identification of the technology needed. In this stage, a country needs to determine its national goals and priorities in light of its internal and external environments. For example, an LDC's national goal could be to (1) develop the agricultural sector, (2) develop certain parts of the industrial sector, or (3) fulfill social needs.

IDENTIFICATION STAGE

The second stage is to determine what technology is needed for each goal identified in the first stage. Technology suitable in one environment is not necessarily suitable in another because of differences in the level of development or other internal conditions. This stage requires the following actions:

1. Identify available managerial capability and what must be done to raise it to a level that can absorb the technology needed. If managerial capability is lacking, the next step is to determine how it can be developed, either by intensive training of locals or bringing in experts.
2. Identify the infrastructure that must be available when the technology is used. The infrastructure includes roads, facilities, and information.
3. Identify the strengths and weaknesses of government regulations and policies and test whether they inhibit or encourage new technology. Regulations should be modified as necessary to make them more attractive to suppliers of new technology.
4. Identify the folkways, mores, or customs of a country that might oppose the introduction of new technology.

SEARCH FOR ALTERNATIVES

The third stage is to search for alternatives to the technology identified in terms of sources and appropriateness. This stage requires identification of the criteria for selection of appropriate technology that satisfies a country's internal and external conditions. The first criterion is to determine a fair price, after a survey of all available sources of the technology. The second criterion is the degree of absorption. Does the capability exist to absorb the technology locally? The third criterion is appropriateness, which addresses the quality of the technology and its supplier. An LDC should establish criteria for the selection of the desired technology from either MNCs or from other sources that can provide similar technology.

EVALUATION STAGE

The fourth stage is to evaluate the alternatives available for acquiring the desired technology. In this stage, the best form of investment is determined based on an LDC's internal and external environment. For example, MNCs are usually reluctant to license their technology except under very profitable conditions. Even if these conditions are met, the technology might not be truly appropriate for a particular developing country. Therefore, an LDC needs to decide whether licensing, a joint venture, or wholly owned subsidiary could be the appropriate form of investment.

SELECTION STAGE

After identifying the type of technology and its sources, the final consideration is how to implement it. The specific actions, programs, policies, timetables, and resources required need to be determined. Sometimes the organization receiving the technology needs to make structural changes. Reward and performance evaluations systems are important in adapting new technology. After adapting the technology and using it for two to three years, it is always important to revisit the entire process to determine whether any changes need to be made.

A firm that is committed to technology transfer, either by supplying technology or acquiring it internationally, encounters many new issues. For example, once a country gains technological advantage, it wants to maintain that advantage. The technology market is very volatile. The need to maintain a competitive advantage in foreign markets is similar to maintaining an advantage in the domestic market. Maintaining advantage is also important in retaining bargaining power against government control policies. Trademarks and patents also serve to maintain advantage. An extensive research capability is one of the most important tools to develop new technologies and continue improvements.

Although technology is considered to be an asset, a firm's research and development (R&D) capability comprises its true technological advantage. It is not uncommon for host countries to pressure MNCs to establish R&D facilities in addition to production facilities. Foreign R&D facilities make a firm more competitive in both home and host country markets. R&D operations can be very helpful in the technology transfer process. Products can be made or adapted for local conditions, or new products can be developed specifically for foreign markets.

The final aspect of technology transfer is control. Donor countries expect a higher return on investment (ROI), and usually are reluctant to share their advanced technology. National security is always a major reason why advanced nations are protective of their technologies. Last but not least, unless the transferred technologies are properly adapted, efforts spent toward the transfer are wasted.

Technology Transfer to Less Developed Countries

Jerry Ladman[1] brings a different perspective to the subject of technology transfer to the less developed countries (LDCs). The role of the United Nations in particular has been highlighted in this section.

The importance of technology in the growth of civilizations has been amply recognized by historians who have labeled progressive stages of human development as the Stone, Bronze, Machine, and Atomic Ages. Yet within each of these ages, the fruits of available technology have been unevenly distributed. This has led to a somewhat uneven pattern of growth of the different civilizations and regions of the world. Thus, over the course of history, technology in the form of both consumer and producer goods has tended to be transferred from those countries that have developed the technology to those which did not have it.

During the Industrial Revolution, technological development was concentrated in Western Europe and the United States; thus, these regions became centers of manufacturing activities. In sharp contrast, most of the nations of Africa, Asia, and Latin America had experienced little technological advancement except in mining and some agricultural production. In accordance with the principle of comparative advantage, trade of manufactured goods and raw materials developed between the industrial nations and the primary materials–producing countries. This pattern continued well into the twentieth century. Technology transfer in this stage was basically in the form of introducing consumer goods developed in the advanced Western countries via trade to the primary materials–producing countries. To a much lesser extent some production technology was transferred through foreign investment and the immigration of entrepreneurs and skilled labor.

In the latter part of the nineteenth century the technologically advanced countries began to undertake more direct foreign investment—and the associated technology transfer—in the poorer countries. Involved were not only raw materials production, but also transportation, communication, and public utilities. The major transfers of technology continued, however, as a result of international trade.

A major change in this trend occurred when the LDCs that produce raw materials realized, as a result of the severe shocks of World Wars I and II and the Great Depression, that they could not rely on the export of primary products as the engine of growth of their economies. They then turned to industrialization and constructed protective tariffs to encourage domestic manufacturing under programs of import substitution.

The response was twofold. First, foreign firms, which had identified markets in these countries through their previous exports, immediately jumped the tariff barriers and began local production of the same goods. Second, the domestic firms secured licenses from foreigners for the rights to produce and distribute products which had foreign patents and trademarks. Therefore, in this stage the processes of technology transfer not only continued the pattern of introducing Western culture–style goods to the LDCs, but more importantly, led to the establishment of manufacturing facilities in these countries utilizing the techniques of the Western world. This same pattern continued as the LDCs began to look to regional trade grouping and export markets as additional stimuli for economic growth.

Strong arguments can be developed in favor of a world economic system of trade in accordance with the principle of comparative advantage as well as international movements of resources. Yet, in the last several decades, concern swelled from critics who argued that such a situation has only led to a dependency of the LDCs on the developed countries (DCs) for imported products, export markets, investment capital, and technology. The rise of the multinational corporations (MNCs) in recent years has only served to strengthen this position, since these large firms exhibit such a strong base of economic power and associated political leverage and influence.[2]

In earlier times the question of technology transfer was largely confined to academic papers. In the 1970s the question of technology transfer from the DCs to the LDCs has become an important issue on the international scene. This is especially true since a number of LDCs have passed new and more restrictive legislation on the subject. The reasons for this increasing importance are readily evident. On the one hand, almost all of modern technology has been developed in the DCs. On the other hand, the LDCs recognize the acute need for technological innovation alongside capital investment in their countries in order to increase productivity and generate income and employment. Thus, it is only natural that LDCs should look to the possibilities of foreign aid, foreign investment, and technology transfer from the DCs as a means to foster economic development. Whereas the roles and means of foreign aid and direct foreign investment have long been subject to question and discussion, it is only in recent years that technology transfer has come under scrutiny in international forums.

In response to threatened sovereignty and the alleged abuses of the past, a number of LDCs not only have developed new legislation dealing with technology transfer but also have turned to the solidarity of groups in international forums in order to try to establish a power base for developing and negotiating norms for foreign investment and technology transfer. Examples include: the pronouncements of former Mexican president Luis Echeveria in his Rights of Nations speech before the 1972 United Nations Conference on Trade and Development (UNCTAD) assembly; the pronouncements of the Group 77 LDCs in the UNCTAD; the specific treatment of the subject in Decision 24 of the Andean Group; and the discussion of same in the Articles of Incorporation of the Latin American Economic System (SELA) in 1975. As a consequence, controversy over technology transfer between DCs and LDCs has come to the fore.

AN OVERVIEW OF THE ISSUES

The purpose of this chapter is to identify and discuss the three key issues that surround the process of technology transfer from the DCs to the LDCs and to examine some of the policy alternatives. First is the issue of the price of technology and the rights of the sellers and buyers of same. This issue captures much of the attention in today's world because it encompasses the current and ongoing negotiations between the DCs and LDCs as well as negotiations involving private industry on both sides with respect to foreign investment and technology transfer. The ominous presence of the relatively new MNCs in combination with a long history of alleged exploitation of LDCs by foreign investors and the DCs has led the LDCs to try to obtain investment and technology on much better terms than in the past. Meanwhile, owners of technology in DCs, long accustomed to having much their own way, are resisting giving up this advantage. Thus, there is considerable ground for negotiation on the terms with which technology will be transferred.

The second issue is considerably more subtle and less clearly understood. It deals with the appropriateness of the technology being transferred. Most technology has been developed in the economic and cultural climate of the DCs. Thus, producers are geared to mass consumption and relatively wealthy society; production techniques reflect the relative scarcity of labor and abundance of capital in the DCs. In contrast, the LDCs have large segments of their populations living in a traditional context under conditions of unemployment and poverty. The relative scarcity of capital and abundance of labor suggests the need for labor-intensive production techniques, precisely the opposite that is generally available for transfer from DCs. Thus, two basic questions must be raised: Is the type of technology being transferred, as embodied in consumer goods, appropriate; and is the type of capital-intensive production technology that is being transferred appropriate?

Rights and Price

The interrelated issues of the property rights of sellers and buyers of technology and the determination of a price for the technology are at the core of new LDCs' technology transfer legislation that is designed to protect the interest of the LDCs. The controversial nature of the laws generates strong feelings on both sides that quickly inflame the points in conflict and hence threaten to create conditions of impasse and seriously hinder the flow of technological knowledge.[3]

On the one hand, foreign owners of technology, such as the MNCs, are casting about the world for opportunities to undertake foreign investment and its associated technological component or to sell their technological knowledge through licensing agreements. The technology available for transfer is typically patented and thus the seller is in the position of having certain monopoly powers over his exclusive information. Therefore, the sellers are in a position of not only being able to select to whom they will transfer the technology but also to negotiate from a position of power in determining the price of the technology and the conditions under which it will be employed.

On the other hand, the LDCs recognize the need for additional technology in their development programs. Under the sting of the alleged exploitation of the past, LDCs' governments are eager to establish norms for technology transfer that, in their view, are more equitable than those of the past. Yet LDCs recognize, in the presence of competition for foreign investment and technology with other countries, that they must not adopt a drastic and rigid posture for fear of losing the interests of foreign suppliers of technology. Thus, the battleground is established. The point essentially revolves around two distinct but interrelated issues: the property rights of both the sellers and buyers of technology and the price as cost of the technology being transferred.

At the heart of both issues is the philosophical question of ownership. Technology is information and as such embodies different characteristics than more tangible property such as physical goods. Technology is not exhaustible; it can be used over and over again. Moreover, many of the ideas contained in a particular technology were not developed by the owner but were gained in part from general knowledge or earlier technologies.[4] Thus, the concept of technology ownership, whether protected by the patents or not, is a philosophical gray area and as a consequence is subject to considerable negotiation with respect to the rights of both buyers and sellers.

ISSUES

There are several major points in dispute. First, what technology will be transferred? The owner is in the position of holding all the cards and he may wish to withhold some and thus not transfer his total stock of technological information. Since the buyer does not have this information, he deals in a partial vacuum and may not realize the extent of the technology, or lack of technology, he is purchasing.

Second, what products will be produced with the technology? Can the seller specify the product line to be limited to certain products or can the buyer use the same technology to produce a wider product line?

Third, what limits can the seller impose on the distribution of this product? Can they be exported? If so, can they compete with the seller's own product lines elsewhere in the world?

Fourth, will the buyer also be required to purchase and use trademarks for the products produced? This represents an additional cost to the purchaser.

Fifth, what rights does the buyer have to resell the technology or to make it available to competitors?

Sixth, and related to all of the above, what is the effective duration of any agreement between the buyer and the seller?

The determination of the price of technology is another murky theoretical issue.[5] At its root is the previously mentioned question of ownership; does the nature of the product suggest that the seller should expect to extract the price that his monopoly position might permit? Besides the debatable point, the price that is determined in the marketplace should be one that is mutually satisfactory to buyer and seller. It can be expected that the marginal returns to the purchaser will be quite high, whereas the marginal cost of selling the technology will be relatively low. Thus, a process of bargaining must take place in order to determine a price between these two positions. Interestingly, however, the buyer is at a bargaining disadvantage because he does not have complete information about the technology he is purchasing. Is it possible that the seller might choose to withhold information? This aspect, in combination with the sheer economic power of many sellers of technology, places the buyer at a severe disadvantage.

Historically, the sellers have, therefore, been able to establish prices very favorable to themselves. Typically, the price of technology under a licensing agreement is based on an initial fee in addition to royalties based on a percentage of gross sales. Royalties of 3 percent of gross sales may appear on the surface to be quite reasonable, but when figured on the basis of the actual value added by the new production in the technology-purchasing country, they may be considerably higher and appear to be out of line. In the case where technology transfer is embodied in direct foreign investment there may be no technology charge per se; but an implicit price exists in terms of the amount of profits taken out of the country directly through repatriation, or indirectly through higher transfer prices and high capitalization technology on the businesses' books. The direct and indirect effects both contribute to an outflow of foreign exchange, and the direct effect creates a lower tax base. The net effect is higher profits for the foreign investor (technology transferred) and higher costs for the host country through lower income and large outflow of foreign exchange.

POLICIES

In light of the basic conflict, broad policy considerations are apparent. First, the LDCs must continue to utilize regional and international groups to espouse their collective interests and to provide a larger base of power to confront the powerful MNCs. This will serve to enhance their bargaining position for both the price and terms of technology transfer.

Second, as exemplified by former Secretary of State Henry Kissinger's 1975 speech to the General Assembly of the United Nations, the DCs must also be willing to work out means to facilitate the technology transfer.[6] A logical outcome will be the gradual establishment, by DCs' and LDCs' collaboration, of a set of general international norms that will provide guidelines for technology transfer. This should be done in such a way as to take into account the interest of both the buyer and the seller and not be heavily biased in favor of the latter, which has been so typical of the past.

Third, individual LDCs must continue to develop technology transfer legislation that is more protective of their own interests, not only in the context of the price and terms of the technology transfer but also the appropriateness of the technology within the context of the country's development plan. Yet, at the same time, the legislation should contain enough flexibility to permit the country to negotiate more liberally for technology that is crucial to its development plan and to permit effective competition with other LDCs that are alternate buyers for the available technology. If such policies are followed, a new era of technology transfer will be attained where there will be a harmonious and mutually advantageous marriage between the buyers and sellers of technology, perhaps on terms that may be less favorable than each might desire, but containing what will be acceptable to both and workable for a long period.

APPROPRIATE TECHNOLOGY

Issue

The issue of the appropriateness of the technology being transferred, unfortunately, does not gain the attention that it deserves. Yet, in many ways it comes to the core of serious and fundamental problems that most LDCs must solve in order to escape their state of underdevelopment. There are two dimensions of the issue—demand and supply. On the demand side is the type of consumer goods that are being transferred to the LDCs. The Western style of culture that is ubiquitously being transplanted around the world, as represented by the products produced, often has the effect of destroying traditional values and supplanting products that are indigenous to LDCs. While, in part, this is desirable, more attention should be given to modifying these products in such a way that will permit these cultures to maintain important aspects of their traditions and thus avoid cultural dependency. Another demand dimension is that many of these modern products have associated capital-intensive production techniques. As a result, their production in LDCs does not lend itself to absorbing labor as would the production of more simple and perhaps traditional products.

On the supply side, appropriate technology deals with production techniques that are more compatible with LDCs' resource endowments in order to get at the serious problems of poverty, unemployment, and income distribution. Recent estimates are that at least 10 percent of the work forces in most LDCs are without jobs and that 25 to 40 percent of those who work are significantly underemployed. Moreover, it is estimated that 67 percent of the population in LDCs is seriously poor and 30 percent destitute.[7] Thus, strong arguments are made to utilize labor-intensive technology in order to create employment and income-earning opportunities in these countries.

The problem, as mentioned previously, is that most available technology from DCs and MNCs is capital intensive due to the resource conditions in those countries. The policy implication is that means should be utilized to develop technologies more suited to the factor endowments of LDCs. A caveat is in order, however. There are some capital-intensive production processes, for example, petroleum refining, for which it is highly improbable that less capital-intensive techniques can be developed or, even if they exist, that they would be economical. Yet, even in these cases there are possibilities of making modifications, such as in handling materials, where more labor could be employed.

POLICY ALTERNATIVES

Generalizations about the policy alternatives for this issue can be broadly grouped under those for LDCs and DCs. LDCs first need to take serious account of this problem by establishing appropriate technology norms in their development plans. The general lack of such norms to date suggests a strong need for enlightenment of their leadership.

Second, LDCs should give strong consideration to doing away with policies such as concessionary interest rates in credit programs that give subsidies to capital-intensive techniques.

Third, LDCs should consider developing technologies of their own both for types of consumer goods and for production processes. Because this type of applied research is very costly, LDCs might look to the programs of international cooperation in order to share the costs for developing technologies that are appropriate and transferable across national boundaries. The international agricultural centers provide a good example of this approach and its benefits.

In the DCs, governments can facilitate the development of appropriate technology in several ways. First, foreign aid and technical assistance can be provided to help the development of such technology. Second, they can estimate research directly through funded research projects or indirectly through incentives to the private sector. Third, they can develop, as has been proposed in the United States, a technology clearing house that could function as a source of technology both for resurrecting obsolete technologies of DCs, which may be nowadays applicable in LDCs, and for cataloging existing technologies in the world in order to make them available to LDCs.

The private sector in DCs can also make a contribution through conscious efforts to develop products and production techniques that are available to LDCs' needs. The small tractor program of Massey Ferguson and television assembly programs of Phillips are examples of what has been done. Perhaps the most important incentive to encourage such research by the private sector is their recognition of a potential market for these products. Thus, if the LDCs effectively demonstrate a need for and exert pressure for such technology, its development will be enhanced.

ECOLOGICAL TECHNOLOGY

This issue is common for both DCs and LDCs. It has become increasingly apparent that the modern world in search of technological advancement has created a new generation of problems through the side effects of pollution and congestion. Thus, considerable recent attention has been directed to modification of production processes and the development of consumer goods and a lifestyle that have less pollutive and congestive effects. Perhaps the most articulate proponent to date has been E. F. Schumacher, whose book *Small Is Beautiful* has received widespread attention.[8]

Another dimension of the problem is that modern technology requires heavy utilization of nonrenewable resources. The doomsday message of the Club of Rome[9] is clear—as the world's population grows and economic advancement occurs, civilization will begin to bump against the constraints of limited resources. Thus, unless technology is altered to use considerably lower coefficients of these resources and to reduce the negative ecological side effects, and unless the rate of population growth is drastically reduced, the world's average level of living will eventually decline.

LDCs could seriously diminish the negative ecological effects of increased production and reduce the rate of consumption of nonrenewable resources if they were to utilize technology that had low pollutive and congestive side effects and low requirements for exhaustible resources. This, however, is a big order on two accounts. First, much of this type of technology is not yet available and it can hardly be expected that LDCs should or would be willing to wait until such a time as it is available to continue their development. Second, where such technology is available, such as smoke arresters on factory chimneys, it is expensive and raises production costs, which would require the use of scarce capital resources that could otherwise be employed in society. The present value of such future benefits may not be very high in a society that is struggling to cope with the more pressing problems of employment and poverty. Indeed, it is probably a rare government that would choose to allocate substantial resources in such a manner.

POLICIES

This is not to suggest that there are no policy alternatives that can be implemented in the meantime. First, as pressures from limited resources and polluting production techniques come to bear more urgently through the world, more emphasis will be given to the development of alternative technologies in the DCs that can in turn be transferred to LDCs. Second, LDCs can utilize policies that are harmonious with both the short-run development goals and long-run ecological goals. Examples are regional development programs to avoid excessive migration to the capital cities; encouragement of labor-intensive technology in rural areas to reduce rural-urban migration; subsidies for mass transportation systems and penalties for single automobiles; and plans for urban centers and industrial sites.

CONCLUSIONS

In the 1990s, technology transfer has emerged as an issue for LDCs. Previously, a transfer of technology both in the form of consumer goods and in production techniques took place through foreign trade, direct foreign investment, and licensing agreements, but under terms that were largely determined by the owners of technology in DCs. In this decade, LDCs have begun to develop norms that would be more favorable to their particular interests. Most of the attention has been directed to the price of the technology and the terms under which it is transferred. While this issue is extremely important in order for the LDCs to reap advantages from technology at a lower cost, longer-term and more subtle issues of the appropriateness of technology and its ecological effects are also emerging.

A number of policy measures dealing with each of the three issues were set forth in this chapter; several major points emerge. First, while the individual LDCs must develop their own plans and provisions for technology transfer, it is important that they continue to group together as they have done in the past decade in order not only to express their concerns collectively but also to form blocks of power that can confront the extreme economic power of the sellers of technology such as the MNCs. Only in this manner will they be able to effectively improve their bargaining position.

Second, part of the responsibility lies with the DCs. They must work to help establish norms for the operations of MNCs that include technology transfer. Also, as part of their foreign assistance programs, they must direct resources toward the development and dissemination of technology that is more appropriate to the resource endowments of LDCs. Moreover, they have a responsibility to develop technology that confronts the ecological and nonrenewable resource problems and that can, in turn, be transferred to LDCs.

Thus, for all three issues, the policy prescription calls for individual as well as collaborative action on the part of both LDCs and DCs. Given the need for the international transfer of resources, including technology, it is in their mutual interests to work together. Although conflicts of interest are bound to arise, such as the current negotiations over price and terms, both LDCs and DCs have sufficient self-interest that they will find means to solve these conflicts and move ahead together to their mutual benefit.

NOTES

1. Jerry R. Ladman, "Technology Transfer to Less Developed Countries," *Arizona Business* 24, no. 8 (October 1977), pp. 15–21. Reprinted with permission from the author and the Center for Business Research, L. William Seidman Research Institute, College of Business, Arizona State University, Tempe, Arizona.

2. See, for example, Osvaldo Sunkel, "The Pattern of Latin American Dependence," paper presented at Conference on the Economic and Financial Relations of Latin America with the Industrialized Countries, held at the Colegio de Mexico, Mexico City, December 6–11, 1971, sponsored by the International Economic Association (mimeographed); and Ronald Muller, "The Multinational Corporation and the Underdevelopment of the Third World," in Charles K. Wilber, ed., *The Political Economy of Development and Underdevelopment* (New York: W.W. Norton, 1973), pp. 186–204.

3. Jose de Cubas, *Technology Transfer and the Developing Nations* (New York: Council for the Americas and Fund for Multinational Management Education, 1974), p. 1.

4. Constantine V. Vaistos, "Bargaining and the Distribution of Returns in the Purchase of Technology by Developing Countries," *Bulletin of Institute of Development Studies* (October 1970), pp. 16–23, reprinted in Gerald M. Meier, *Leading Issues in Economic Development*, 3d ed. (New York: Oxford University Press, 1976), pp. 413–414.

5. Ibid.

6. Henry J. Kissinger, "Global Consensus and Economic Development," speech delivered at Seventh Special Session of the United Nations Special Assembly, September 1, 1975 (Washington, D.C.: U.S. Department of State, Bureau of Public Affairs, Office of Media Services), p. 7.

7. International Labor Office, *Employment, Growth and Basic Needs: A One World Problem* (Geneva: ILO, 1976), pp. 18 and 21.

8. E. F. Schumacher, *Small Is Beautiful* (New York: First Perennial Library Edition, Harper and Row Publishers, 1975).

9. Donella H. Meadows, Dennis L. Meadows, Jorgen Randers, and William W. Beherens III, *The Limits to Growth* (New York: Signet Books by the New American Library, 1972).

Potential Costs of Technology Transfer

This chapter presents Professor Ira Saltz's views on technology transfer. Literature on technology transfer discusses the mutual benefits of technology transfer to both the investing multinational company and to the host Third World country. Indeed, the potential benefits to the host country are great: increased employment, access to new technologies, more capital investment, increased demand for domestically produced goods, less reliance upon imports, and job training. However, these are *potential* benefits, or benefits in theory. The experiences of many Third World countries differ substantially with respect to the degree of benefit. There is a concern among many development economists that the costs of technology transfer may outweigh the benefits in many cases. This chapter explores some of the main factors that decide whether the benefits exceed the costs and some of the theory and evidence that suggests that technology transfer is not always beneficial.

The assumptions of new-classical theory that microeconomic choices made by individual agents would be socially Pareto-optimal as long as there is perfect competition, perfect information, and all externalities are accounted for do not necessarily hold in the aggregate. This is quite probably true for the choice of technology. A particular choice of technology may be appropriate for the individual firm or even the industry as a whole; it may not be appropriate to the society. As such, it may also be helpful to judge technology transfer at the macroeconomic level.

MacDougall (1960) wrote the first major work on technology transfer.[1] He used partial-equilibrium analysis to determine the effects of capital inflows. His book examined the distribution of gains between labor, domestic capital, and foreign capital from capital inflows. He concluded that the host country would gain mainly through taxes on profits generated by foreign firms, through economies of scale, and external economies associated with training and management skills. He also concluded that real wages would rise. Other work from the mainstream quickly followed from MacDougall's (1960) work.

Bos, Sanders, and Secchi (1974) and Bacha (1974) used pure trade theory in a general equilibrium dynamic growth model to determine the effects of capital inflows. Their analysis, however, was the first major work to consider the importance of comparing the effects of technology transfer in light of the alternatives. Borrowing from Streeten and others, they list the main alternatives to foreign direct investment (FDI) as:

1. Raising the capital and other resources domestically.
2. Borrowing from abroad, as well as hiring managers and engineers through licensing agreements.
3. Engage in joint ventures with foreign firms.
4. Import the good.
5. Forego the good for the present.

It can be pointed out that their list may represent unrealistic alternatives. Many foreign firms are unwilling to license their technology or engage in joint ventures when other developing countries may offer more profitable arrangements. Joint ventures were relatively uncommon until Japanese multinationals started engaging in joint ventures in the late 1960s and early 1970s (Sekiguchi 1979).

Borrowing from abroad may also be unrealistic or a rather limited alternative. Multinational firms, whose parent companies were well established in developed countries, have sizable advantages in capital markets (because they represent less risk and possess marketing and managerial advantages) over a fledgling company in a developing country. It has been found that 88 percent of the capital used by MNCs was raised in the local markets (United Nations 1974). Vernon (1974) also cites evidence that in 1964, for example, U.S. foreign direct investment increased by $3.3 billion worldwide, but only $565 million of that came from U.S. funds. Given that much foreign direct investment is raised from domestic funds and that they repatriate profits, foreign direct investment in many cases causes a net capital outflow.[2] Further evidence of this is cited in Bos, Sanders, and Secchi (1974), which showed that outflow of profits back to the United States exceeded the level of new investment for each year from 1965 to 1969. Included in the new investment was reinvested earnings so that the outflow even further exceeded the inflow. If foreign direct investment primarily comes about by raising capital in the host country's market, then the presence of foreign direct investment may simply redistribute capital from labor-intensive, or employment-generating industries, to capital-intensive industries creating a net loss of employment.

Bos, Sanders, and Secchi (1974) list the potential measurable gains from technology transfer as an increase in GNP and an increase in the balance of payments. The potential gains in GNP have to be weighed against both the potential losses and the possible gains from the alternatives listed above. They break up the possible gains into two categories, direct and indirect. The direct gains include the increased output, wages, royalties, and taxes when the output was not attainable in the alternatives. Earlier studies had found sizable gains to the host country from foreign direct investment because of huge royalty payments. However, royalty payments were more the exception than the rule, resulting primarily from investment in extractive industries, which comprises a very small fraction of all fdi today.

The negative direct effects Bos, Sanders, and Secchi (1974) list are the distortions to prices created by high rates of protectionism and monopolization. It may turn out that, due to these price distortions, capital and certain other prices may not reflect their actual scarcity causing their overconsumption. For example, if foreign firms can easily raise capital because of their creditworthiness, then this gives the illusion that capital is not scarce in the country. Another negative effect may be the depletion of natural resources. Many foreign firms extracted minerals as fast as they could without regard to their future availability.

The indirect effects include the creation or destruction of forward and backward linkages, terms of trade effects, and the preemption of domestic investment. Forward linkages are defined as the creation of goods by the foreign firm that are inputs to domestic producers. Backward linkages is the demand for domestically produced inputs by the foreign firm. The potential gains of FDI are expanded if the economic activity increases the demand for other industries' goods in the host country. For example, potential losses arise if the multinational's production process does not create linkages and the best alternative's activity would have done so.

It was also noted that potential negative terms of trade effects were possible as a result of excessive extraction that caused the prices of many of the developing countries' natural resources to fall. In addition, the parent company of many of the foreign firms in the host countries explicitly forbade or limited the exports of the foreign firm. Also, the foreign firm may have a greater propensity to import inputs than a domestic firm.

Bos, Sanders, and Secchi (1974) also point out that the advantage of foreign firms to raise capital in the host country's market may result in a situation where domestic firms are left without funding for their investment projects, especially given the shortage of capital. This is known as the preemption of investment. There was also concern that there would be no direct output effect if the foreign firm just took over a domestic firm. In fact, the resulting monopolization could lead to a fall in output.

Although the model set up by Bos, Sanders, and Secchi (1974) was the most detailed attempt at that time to account for all effects of FDI, their cost-benefit analysis was severely hampered by a lack of sufficient de-segregated data and the limiting assumptions they were forced to make. Their results followed logically from their limiting assumptions. The most limiting assumption was that demand is supply-determined, since they calculated consumption as a residual of income–savings–taxes. Also, they were forced to assume equal export and import propensities of foreign and domestic firms.

Baldwin (1970) and Chipman (1971) studied this same topic using the Hecksher-Ohlin trade analysis. They concluded that capital inflows increased the capital-intensity of production both directly and indirectly through the effect of raising the return on capital. Vaitsos (1974b) evaluated the effects of technology transfer in a different perspective. He faulted the earlier works for treating foreign direct investment the same as any other type of capital inflow. The crux of Vaitsos's (1974b) work is that technology transfer represents a total package that includes the choice of technology, management technique, and control that does not accompany other forms of capital inflows. In addition, the technological choice made by foreign firms would affect the host country's demand for intermediate goods. Vaitsos (1974b) presents evidence from Chile that the inflow of FDI precludes linkages that may have been formed in the alternate. For example, the high tariffs granted MNCs may reduce the competitiveness of import markets. Table B.1 illustrates some examples from Chile. It lists the percentage of total payments for imports by the sector paid to the country listed in the center column.

By employing technologies that may require specific skills or inputs that may not be available in the host country market, multinationals have the power to create monopolies. The theory of technological monopolies was first discussed in Merhav (1969). However, Vaitsos (1974b) extended this by demonstrating that multinationals, through their pricing policies and control of intermediate goods and available resources, are able to maintain their monopoly power.

Another practice of multinationals that diminishes their benefit to the host country is transfer pricing. Transfer pricing is the overpricing of the imported inputs and underpricing of the exported product, thereby shifting profits from the host country to the home country. It has been conceded in the literature that transfer pricing exists. However, the degree of transfer pricing had rarely been addressed before Vaitsos's study

Table B.1
Chile's Imports by Sector, Countries, and Percent

Sector	Countries	Percent
Tobacco	United Kingdom	100.0
Industrial chem.	West Germany, Switzerland	96.6
Other chemicals	U.S.A., Switzerland, and West Germany	92.0
Petroleum and coal products	U.S.A. and United Kingdom	100.0
Rubber products	U.S.A.	99.9
Non-metallic minerals	U.S.A.	97.0
Metallic products	U.S.A.	94.0
Non-electric machinery	U.S.A.	98.7
Electric equipment	Holland, U.S.A., Spain	92.0
Transport equipment	France, Switzerland	89.0

Source: G. Oxman, "La Balanza de Pagos Technologicos de Chile," mim., September 1971.

(1974b). He referred to several studies being conducted for Chile and Colombia that showed high rates of overpricing of imports and underpricing of exports. He defined the percentage of overpricing of imports as:

FOB price in purchasing country − FOB price in rest of world × 100

R.O.W. FOB price

where FOB is the price "free on board." He found that in most cases, the foreign firms in Colombia and Chile, especially, had significantly higher rates of overpricing than the domestic firms. For example, in Colombia, foreign firms in pharmaceuticals overpriced by 155 percent compared with only 19 percent for domestic firms and in rubber the foreign firms overpriced imports by 40 percent compared to 0 percent for domestic firms.

Another fault with much of the prior work is that the notion of return on investment is cloudy, at best. Multinationals, through transfer pricing, reallocation of fixed costs, research and development, and other accounting tricks can hide actual rates of return. Vaitsos (1974b) points out that many foreign firms in Latin America were reporting heavy losses, but continued to operate, which does not follow logically from standard economic theory. If a venture is not profitable, in the long run, the firm will exit that industry. Further, other foreign firms waited anxiously for the permission to enter the domestic market. Again, this behavior is inconsistent with standard economic theory. Vaitsos (1974b) estimates that if one includes in the rate of return on investment not only the reported profits but also the royalties, the profitability of FDI is grossly understated in the mainstream literature. Remembering that most of the capital used by foreign firms is raised in the domestic market, technology transfer quite clearly causes a decrease in capital through transfer pricing, royalties, other factor payments, and monopoly rents, in many cases. If this is true, it invalidates one of the major benefits that technology transfer supposedly offers the host country.

This *total package* approach led Vaitsos (1974a) to conclude that certain aspects of foreign direct investment can be beneficial, but the distortions created by the whole package could actually cause technology transfer to be detrimental. If tariff protection and monopolization lead to higher rates of return for foreign capital, then there would be lower rates of return to domestic factors, causing an income flow from the poor host country to the richer home country. The high rates of return on foreign capital would also perpetuate the substitution of capital for labor, increasing the capital-intensity of production throughout the economy. These distortions of factor prices will lead developing countries to stray from their comparative advantage and increase their dependency on the developed world through increased import demand for capital goods and through explicit agreements to limit the production of certain goods for export. Mahler finds a correlation between the level of FDI and the 3-country concentration ratio of a developing country's trade.[3] Saltz (1992) finds evidence that the share of imports in GDP is positively correlated with the share of foreign direct investment in GDP. Further, Saltz and Cebula (1993) show that the capital-intensity of technology is also positively correlated with the share of foreign direct investment in GDP.

Other studies have also dealt with the *appropriateness* of the technology issue. Rhadu (1973) for Pakistan; Agarwal (1976); Morley and Smith (1974) for Brazil among others found that MNCs tended not to adapt their technologies and used *inappropriate* technologies. However, several other studies found that the foreign firms' technology did not differ from those of the local firms. In response, Chen (1983) and others concluded that in some cases the multinational's technology had been copied by the local firms in order to compete, giving the appearance of adaptation by the MNC. Jenkins (1991) concludes that all of these studies may be flawed by their assumption that the behavior of local firms is not independent of the behavior of dominant foreign firms. Chen (1983) also found that many Japanese multinationals did use more labor-intensive technologies in their foreign subsidiaries.[4] This is consistent with the above findings because in countries like Korea, the Philippines, Taiwan, and Thailand, Japanese firms comprised a relatively high share of the foreign firms operating in these countries.

However adaptive or nonadaptive multinationals seemed to be, the conclusion of Parry (1980) is that those foreign firms typically invested in more capital-intensive industries. In this case, the small difference in capital-intensity of technology between local and foreign firms is not surprising. It is quite possible that the presence of foreign firms causes the more capital-intensive sectors of manufacturing to expand more rapidly than the labor-intensive sectors, thus skewing growth toward economic activities with less growth potential for employment. This issue was studied by Saltz. There was some evidence that the shares of the relatively capital-intensive industries in total manufacturing were higher the higher the share of foreign direct investment in GDP.

Even if foreign firms use more capital-intensive technologies, there may be a net creation of employment because of the linkage effects of multinationals. However, Lall and Streeten (1977) find that multinationals tend to invest in industries with high import propensities, thus reducing the linkage effect and exacerbating the balance of payments problem. Merhav (1969) concludes that foreign direct investment is a transmission mechanism having an overall effect of driving out labor-intensive growth and replacing it with capital-intensive growth.

CONCLUSION

The focus of this chapter has been on the potentially negative effects of technology transfer on the host Third World country. However, this is not to imply that *all* technology transfer is harmful or that Third World countries should not encourage technology transfer. What this chapter is attempting to bring to light are the conditions under which the costs of technology transfer can exceed the benefits and that host countries must carefully examine the conditions under which foreign firms operate.

NOTES

1. MacDougall is credited as the first major work by Lall and Streeten (1977).

2. For example, a study done by the Commonwealth Club titled "U.S. Private Investment: What Should Be Its Future Role in Inter-American Development?" cites that the Latin American countries were complaining that the level of re-

patriation exceeded the inflow of foreign direct investment. *The Commonwealth,* March 29, 1976.

3. The three-country concentration is the percentage of all exports shipped to the three leading recipients of a country's exports.

4. This coincides with the findings related to Japanese FDI reported in the *World Development Report, 1985* and with the results reported in this chapter.

The Reciprocal Distribution Paradigm

This chapter presents a new idea regarding global technology transfer. This idea uses distribution as a new mode of transfer. In today's complex global markets, access to distribution channels or lack of it can make or break a firm's global market penetration ambitions. Regardless of how well a product is made or how well the brand is known internationally, unless the product/brand is distributed properly through appropriate distribution channels in other countries, the firm's global marketing objectives cannot be met. Also, when a firm's traditional entry strategies such as exporting, licensing, manufacturing, joint venture, and strategic alliances fail to produce desired results, the reciprocal distribution idea can be tried as a viable strategy.

In international markets, often the distribution problem gets complex for two reasons: (1) too many tariff and nontariff barriers, and (2) a nationalistic fervor in some countries that discourages importation of foreign goods into that country. In addition, there are other factors such as differences in the channels of distribution from country to country in their set-up and contractual terms, and conditions that compound the difficulty. While the channels may vary within countries, there are also striking differences in the number and types of channels available among countries. To illustrate this complexity, consider the case of Procter and Gamble's difficulties in entering the tough Japanese market. In order to enter the Japanese market, Procter and Gamble has to meander through one of the most complex distribution labyrinths in the world. First, it has to sell its products to a general wholesaler, and from there the products have to journey through a product wholesaler, a product specialty wholesaler, a regional wholesaler, a local wholesaler, and eventually to retailers. So many layers of distribution channels result in price escalation, that is, doubling or tripling of the price over the importer's price (Kotler 1991). This is a disadvantage to a foreign producer to compete with locally made products of similar quality selling at lower prices than the imports.

The channels for industrial product markets, however, might be somewhat less complicated and simpler than that of consumer products. But, even in the case of industrial products, influential producers of industrial goods in other countries may block entry of industrial products into their markets unless they (the local producers) have something to gain from allowing a foreign producer to market its products in the host country. Under these circumstances, the reciprocal distribution (RD) is a good fit. It is particularly a recommended entry alternative into the markets of emerging economies of Eastern Europe, Russia, and developing economies. The purpose of this chapter is to examine how reciprocal distribution can be an effective entry tool to expand into global markets. The circumstances encountered by firms entering RD arrangements are evaluated.

As shown in Figure C.1, the RD model is simple. In its simplest form, it is saying "you distribute my goods and I will distribute yours." A producer/distributor, say X in Country A, can do business with producers and distributors Y, U, and V in Countries B and C, respectively, on a variety of products on a reciprocal distribution basis. The relationships could be single or multiple depending on the opportunities. This type of arrangement is less cumbersome and more productive than other entry strategies such as direct investment, joint venture, licensing, and strategic alliance.

RD is different from "piggybacking" in that a company such as General Electric, for example, agrees to distribute merchandise of overseas firms in U.S. markets. General Electric accepts products that are noncompetitive and complementary, adding to its basic distribution strength. Most piggyback arrangements are undertaken when a firm is trying to fill out its product line or keep its distribution channels for seasonal items functioning throughout the year. Companies may work either on an agency or merchant basis, but the greatest volume of purchases is handled directly on an ownership (merchant) purchase-resale arrangement (Cateora 1993, pp. 450–452).

STRATEGIC ALLIANCE

RD is different from strategic alliance. A strategic alliance between two organizations is an agreement to cooperate to achieve one or more common strategic objectives. It can mean collaborative relationships between two companies at the same level in the distribution channel (Cravens

Figure C.1
A Reciprocal Distribution Paradigm

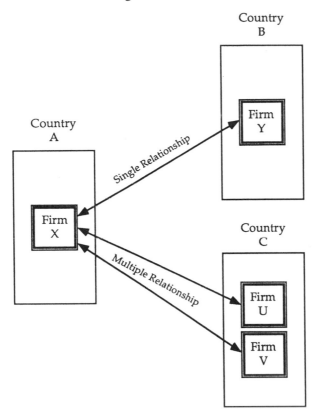

1994, p. 73). It can also be a collaborative relationship between two producers, as in the case of General Motors and Toyota, who manufacture
and market the Geo line of cars in the United States.

One such successful alliance is General Electric's jet engine partnership
Snecm, a French government–controlled aerospace company. Formed in
1974 to help General Electric sell aircraft engines in Europe, the alliance
was successful for both partners.

There are failures in strategic alliance as well. An alliance that did not
work was that of AT&T and Olivetti & Company, the Italian office equipment producer. AT&T was to sell Olivetti's personal computers in the
United States and Olivetti to market AT&T's computers and telecommunications in Italy. This alliance has failed due to lack of marketing
coordination between the two firms. Also, successful alliances are difficult to achieve because of shifts in strategic requirements of the participants; lack of clear decision-making responsibility; conflicts of objectives,

cultures, and styles of management; and the decline of long-term interest on the success of the alliance from either of the parties (Cravens 1994, p. 75).

RECIPROCAL DISTRIBUTION

Compared to the tightly set contractual arrangement of a strategic alliance, RD operates based on a mutual need and understanding. There may not be any legal agreements between the parties, at least in the initial stages.

Benefits

The expected benefits of RD are as follows:

• It is less expensive compared to other methods of entry,
• It has less paperwork,
• There are less red tape and bureaucratic delays,
• RD is good for horizontal technology transfer,
• It is a good method for reverse technology transfer,
• It is simple compared to strategic alliance,
• There are fewer legal hassles with RD,
• It does not have negative political implications,
• It works particularly well in business-to-business and industrial marketing situations,
• It produces synergy for the participants.

Limitations

First, there must be a mutual need for both parties to cooperate. Otherwise, RD arrangements will fail. Second, both parties should equally benefit. Neither of them should think the other is getting more benefit out of the arrangement. Finally, resolving disputes will be next to impossible, since there are no world courts to resolve international business disputes.

SEEKING RD ARRANGEMENTS

Several venues are available to find foreign contacts for RD arrangement. One can contact the U.S. Department of Commerce offices, foreign consulates in the United States, foreign consulates in other countries, international management consultants, trade associations, and the International Chamber of Commerce for information and opportunities for parties to meet and network through common contacts like multinational banks, insurance firms, advertising agencies, freight forwarders, and export/import agents. Second, international trade fairs can provide an excellent opportunity for parties to meet and establish contacts and then work on the RD idea further. Finally, advertisements in trade journals and business magazines can be another venue for those seeking RD arrangements.

HOW THE STRATEGY WORKS

As stated earlier, RD is the exchange of distribution and marketing systems and expertise between two firms in different world markets, each of which offers products that require the marketing planning and execution expertise that the RD partner has developed. The products may or may not be complementary in function. Many financial arrangements are possible, including barter to the extent that each firm's sales to and purchases from the partner are equal. Under an RD arrangement, Firm 1 in Country A agrees to distribute products from Firm 2 in Country B and distribute them in Country A for a return of similar favor.

Thus, both firms profit by enhancing their total marketing productivity through distributing each other's products in each other's markets. The partners may be producers, distributors, or one of each. In the developed country the RD partner sometimes can be a distributor. However, it is better suited for a producer who wishes to export his products and import products that complement his existing product mix to reciprocate. Chrysler, for example, imports and sells Mitsubishi Colt cars in the United States. In return, Mitsubishi sells Chrysler-made cars in Japan.

Larsen and Tubro of India, an electric gear manufacturer, may seek distribution tie-up with Square D, an American manufacturer of electrical equipment. Each firm distributes products of the other, complementing its product lines. Larsen and Tubro can "brand label" Square D products as its own in India and market them through its own distributive network while Square D similarly brand labels and distributes Larsen and Tubro's products in the United States

Another hypothetical example can be that a Brazilian electrical manufacturer might import General Electric's one h.p. motors; in return General Electric imports Brazilian electrical bulbs and labels them as General Electric's brand. The Brazilian firm still produces and markets its own one h.p. motors and sells the imported version to a local refrigerator manufacturing firm that likes the General Electric motor for its higher quality and performance.

Two notions underlie the attractiveness of RD as an entry strategy. First, it is easy to reach the host countries' ports of entry. The difficult part, however, is moving from the ports to the end users' receiving docks or the consumers' homes. The process of reaching the port requires dealing with many regulations, rules, tariff and nontariff barriers, and logistical complexities. The host country's channels of distribution link imported products from the port of entry to the final market destination. Navigating that channel is a major problem in successful market entry (Martin et al. 1983; Rabino 1980; and Racine and Ford 1982). The channel may be structured differently than the home market channel or it may simply be primitive. Operating in it requires dealing with managerial instabilities, inconsistencies and ambiguities that are endemic in a fragmented system of independently managed organizations. Required skills are learned through long-term exposure to cultural, managerial, and personal nuances of the participants.

The second notion underlying the attractiveness of RD is closely related to the first. In an RD deal, both partners bring their individual expertise in dealing with the local market and market infrastructure. They use this local knowledge to help a foreign partner. In effect, the partners are leveraging their local expertise into international marketing. To put it another way, the RD deal is creating an "international value" for the partners' local expertise.

The logic underlying RD is different from that of countertrade. Consequently, most problems in countertrade do not occur in RD (Welt 1982). RD begins with both partners viewing the RD transaction as an opportunity to use their local skills to generate a profit opportunity in international trade.

When we view RD as an entry strategy for developed country markets, the initial moves must come from the developing country. Thus, a firm with limited resources faces the task of analyzing and evaluating opportunities in large and complex markets. Then it must evaluate potential partners and choose one. The method of study and evaluation, therefore, must be comprehensive, but modest. Three steps must be followed:

1. After choosing a product that can be produced in the developing country, analyze the end-use market in the developed host country's market. This can be accomplished through secondary sources. The study should focus on producers in the end-user market. These producers are the potential RD partners.

2. After identifying partners in the host country, find out their interest regarding products. This step builds the ability to offer a partner access to the developing country market. To keep the cost of this step low, potential partners can be identified as types of firms, then specific firms.

3. Armed with an understanding of the most attractive routes to the end-use developed market and with an offer of access to an attractive developing mar-

ket, the producer can identify key producers in another country and begin negotiations with them.

The notion of synergistically combining marketing and distribution know-how is not new. Much of the criticism of it is aimed at the aspect of motivating potential importers to use their expertise to participate in RD (Lowenstein 1981; Martin et al. 1985; Walsh 1985). Often, the opening of reciprocal distribution channels is a stated objective. In some it is the primary objective. Here are some examples:

1. Clark Equipment and Volvo joined forces to capitalize on each other's construction and mining equipment distribution channels (*Business Week*, 1985).
2. Coca-Cola entered the Yugoslavian market with an understanding to market wine produced by its Yugoslavian partner in the U.S. markets (Martin et al. 1985). Most important, both firms have the marketing expertise and channel structure in place to open their local markets to each other. Coca-Cola exports to Yugoslavia and makes profit by distributing its partner's wine in the United States. In turn, the Yugoslavian partner earns hard currency to pay for imports of Coke syrup. Also, it shares profits with Coca-Cola as a Coke bottler in Yugoslavia.

Small companies also are setting up distribution-oriented international agreements. These are more difficult to identify as small firms do not usually receive as much press coverage as the large firms. Nevertheless, two examples are found in the linear actuator and the forging businesses.

3. A Cleveland company produces medium-to-large-sized linear actuators (e.g., geared mechanisms that convert rotary motion to linear motion) in inch dimensions. To fill out its line with metric actuators, it worked with a German producer. The latter needed inch actuators for the replacement market on imported machines.
4. The forging example is identical to the above. Another Cleveland company that produces precision forging needed a line of large forging. It struck a deal with a Brazilian producer, who needed a source of precision forging.

Kahler lists the following additional examples (1983, p. 172):

5. Sony, the Japanese electronic company, sells U.S. and European products in Japan. It established International Housewares to distribute for Whirlpool Corporation; Schick, Inc.; Regal Ware, Inc.; Heath, Inc.; and other U.S. firms. Sony provides a detailed knowledge of the Japanese market, effective promotion effort, and complete servicing for products it represents.
6. Colgate-Palmolive, a U.S. firm, uses its marketing knowledge and distribution system to meet consumer products for many U.S. and foreign firms. It buys razors and blades from Wilkinson Sword Company in Britain and distributes

them in the United States, Canada, and Scandinavia. Herkel of Germany uses Colgate to distribute Pritt glue sticks.

7. A plywood door manufacturing company in the United States finds a door lock manufacturer in Germany interested in the distribution of the American manufacturer's door in Germany, provided the American firm distributes door locks made by the German manufacturer in the United States. The U.S. firm must find ways to distribute the German-made door locks in the United States.

As the wide variety of above examples illustrates, RD fits well in distributing both consumer and industrial products, depending on the circumstances and opportunities available in global marketing. However, RD arrangements between two industrial producers may be simpler and efficient.

CONCLUSION: STRATEGY IMPLICATIONS

In an increasingly turbulent world where mutual trust among countries is scarce and long-term relationships are difficult to make due to constant changes in the marketplace, the reciprocal distribution (RD) is a timely idea. The reciprocal distribution arrangement will work well because each business will work for its self-interest as long as the relationship lasts. There is plenty of anecdotal evidence for RD-oriented international arrangements. Ryans and Mitchell (1986) report that 12 percent of their survey respondents had reciprocal international distribution arrangements. They also report about the same proportions of firms were planning to consider such arrangements. Although the RD idea makes sense a priori, further research is needed to find out how many U.S. firms in fact have RD-type arrangements with firms in other countries. What are the details of such arrangements? What can other firms learn from these arrangements? Without doubt, an in-depth study of the RD arrangements would help immensely to improve the marketing productivity and efficacy of firms involved in global marketing.

References

Agarwal, J. P. (1976). "Factor Proportions in Foreign and Domestic Firms in Indian Manufacturing." *Economic Journal* 86, no. 343, pp. 589–594.

Alkhafaji, Abbass F. (1995). *Competitive Global Management: Principles and Strategies*. Delray Beach, FL: St. Lucie Press.

Amba Rao, Sita C. (1993). "Multinational Corporate Social Responsibility, Ethics, Interactions, and Third World Governments: An Agenda for the 1990s." *Journal of Business Ethics* 12 (July), pp. 553–572.

Amidon Rogers, D. M. (1989). "Entrepreneurial Approaches to Accelerate Technology Commercialization," in K. D. Walters, ed., *Entrepreneurial Management*. Cambridge, MA: Ballinger, 1989.

Amsalem, Michael A. (1983). *Technology Choice in Developing Countries*. Cambridge, MA: MIT Press.

ANVAR (1989). Rapport d'Activite. Paris, France: ANVAR.

Armstrong, Robert W. (1992). "An Empirical Investigation of International Marketing Ethics: Problems Encountered by Australian Firms." *Journal of Business Ethics* 11 (June), pp. 161–172.

Armstrong, Robert W., Bruce W. Stening, John K. Ryans, Larry Marks, and Michael Mayo (1990). "International Marketing Ethics: Problems Encountered by Australian Firms." *European Journal of Marketing* 24, pp. 5–17.

Atkinson, John W. (1977). "Motivation for Achievement," in T. Blass, ed., *Personality Variables in Social Behavior*. Hillsdale, NJ: Erlbaum Associates, 1977, pp. 25–108.

Atkinson, John W., and Norman T. Feather (1966). *A Theory of Achievement Motivation*. New York: Wiley.

Atkinson, John W., and Joel O. Raynor (1974). *Motivation and Achievement*. Washington, DC: Winston.

Bacha, E. L. (1974). "Foreign Capital Inflow and the Output Growth Rate of the Recipient Country." *Journal of Development Studies* 22, pp. 374–381.

Baldwin, R. E. (1970). "International Trade in Inputs and Outputs." *American Economic Review* 6, no. 2 (May), pp. 34–42.

Banerjee, Tridib, and Sanjay Chakravorty (1994). "Calcutta's Planning Experience." *Journal of the American Planning Association* 60, no. 1 (Winter), pp. 71–83.

Baranson, Jack (1969). *Industrial Technologies for Developing Economics*. New York: Praeger.

——— (1981). *Japanese Challenge to U.S. Industry*. Lexington, MA: Lexington Books, D. C. Heath & Company.

Barnet, Richard, and Ronald E. Muller (1974). *Global Reach*. New York: Simon and Schuster.

Bartels, Robert (1967). "A Model for Ethics in Marketing." *Journal of Marketing* 1 (January), pp. 20–26.

Bass, Bernard M. (1979). *Assessment of Managers: An International Comparison*. Riverside, NJ: The Free Press.

Behrman, Jack N. (1978). "International Technology Flows for Development: Suggestions for U.S. Government and Corporate Initiatives," in Jairam Ramesh and Charles Weiss, Jr., eds., *Mobilizing Technology for World Development*. New York: Praeger, 1979, pp. 119–127.

Berkstresser, Gordon A., III, and Kazuo Takeuchi (1983). *Productivity and Quality: Conceptual Differences between Japan and America*. Special pamphlet published by Tokyo Keizai University, No. 129.

Bhagwati, J., R. Brecher, C. Dinopolous, and M. Srinivasan (1987). "Quid Pro Quo Foreign Investment and Welfare: A Political-Economy–Theoretical Model." *Journal of Development Economics* 27, nos. 1–2 (October), pp. 27–40. Special Issue: International Trade, Investment, Macro Policies and History: Essays in Memory of Carlos F. Diaz-Alejandro.

Billerbeck, K., and Y. Yasugi (1979). *Private Direct Foreign Investment in Developing Countries*. World Bank Staff Working Paper No. 348.

Bos, A., D. Sanders, and P. Secchi (1974). *Private Foreign Investment in Developing Countries: A Quantitative Study on the Macroeconomic Effects*. Dordrecht, Holland: D. Reidel Publishing Company.

Bower, D. J. (1991). *Report of a Study-Visit to Japan, 1981*. Japan Information Service. London: The Royal Society.

Business Week (1985). "Clark and Volvo Combine Units." February 4, p. 40.

Business Week (1994). "NIST: More than Weights and Measures." December 19, p. 75.

Buskirk, Bruce D., Allan C. Reddy, and Edward T. Popper (1994). "Planning Market Development in High-Tech Firms." *Technovation* 14, no. 8, pp. 493–502.

Campbell, R. McConnell, and Stanley L. Brue (1990). *Economics*, 11th ed. New York: McGraw-Hill.

Cateora, Philip (1983). *International Marketing*, 5th ed. Homewood, IL: Irwin.

——— (1993). *International Marketing*, 8th ed. Homewood, IL: Irwin.

Caves, Richard E. (1974). "Multinational Firms, Competition and Productivity in Host Country Markets." *Economica* 41, no. 162 (May), pp. 16–24.

Cavusgil, S. Tanner, and John R. Nevin (1983). *International Marketing: An Annotated Bibliography*. Chicago: American Marketing Association.

Center for Applied Economic Research (1980). *The Role of Transnational Corporations in the Developing ESCAP Region.* Paper No. 10, September.

CEST. Center for Exploration of Science and Technology (1991). *Annual Review.* London.

Chase-Dunn, Christopher (1975). "The Effects of International Economic Dependence on Development and Inequality: A Cross-National Study." *American Sociological Review* 40, no. 6 (December), pp. 87–99.

Chen, Edward K. Y. (1983). *Multinational Corporations, Technology, and Employment.* Sarasota, FL: St. Martin's Press.

Chipman, J. (1971). "International Trade with Capital Mobility: A Substitution Theorem," in J. Bhagwati et al., eds., *Trade, Balance of Payments and Growth.* Amsterdam: North-Holland.

Chonko, Lawrence B., and Shelby D. Hunt (1985). "Ethics and Marketing Management: An Empirical Examination." *Journal of Business Research* 13, pp. 329–338.

Cohen, Jeffrey, Laurie Pant, and David Sharp (1993). "A Validation and Extension of a Multidimensional Ethics Scale." *Journal of Business Ethics* 12, pp. 13–26.

Contractor, Farok J., and Tagi Sagafi-Negad (1982). "International Technology Transfer: Major Issues and Policy Responses." *Journal of International Business Studies* 12 (Fall), pp. 113–135.

Corden, W. M. (1974). "The Theory of International Trade," in John H. Dunning, ed., *Economic Analysis and the Multinational Enterprise.* London: George Allen & Unwin, Ltd.

Coy, Peter, Sharon Moshavi, Geri Smith, and Gary McWilliams (1994). "There's More Than One Way to Play Leapfrog." *Business Week*, November 18, pp. 162–164.

Cravens, David W. (1994). *Strategic Marketing*, 4th ed. Burry Ridge, IL: Irwin.

Cunningham, Robert D., and Yasin K. Sarayrah (1994). "The Human Factor in Technology Transfer." *International Journal of Public Administration* 17, no. 8 (July), pp. 419–437.

Davidson, William H. (1980). *Experience Effects in International Investment and Technology Transfer.* Ann Arbor: University of Michigan Press.

de la Torre (1974). "Foreign Investment and Export Dependency." *Economic Development and Cultural Change* 23, no. 1 (October), pp. 133–150.

Department of Trade and Industry (DTI) (1989). *Report of the Interdepartmental Group of the DTI on Intellectual Property.* September. London.

Desruisseaux, Paul (1994). "Renewal of China's Trading Status Angers Some, But Many Are Glad Exchanges Won't Be Disrupted." *The Chronicle of Higher Education*, June 8, pp. 40, A3.

Dorfman, N. (1983). "Rente 128: The Development of Regional High Technology Economy." *Research Policy* 12, pp. 299–316.

Dubinsky, Alan J., and Barbrara Loken (1989). "Analytical Ethical Decision Making in Marketing." *Journal of Business Research* 9, no. 2, pp. 83–107.

Duby, J. J. (1985). "France," in M. Bieber, ed., *Government, Universities, and Industries.* London: Economic Publications.

Dunning, John H., ed. (1971a). *Economic Analysis and the Multinational Enterprise.* London: George Allen & Unwin, Ltd.

———— (1971b). *The Multinational Enterprise*. London: George Allen & Unwin, Ltd.

———— (1985). *Multinational Enterprise, Economic Structure, and International Competitiveness*. New York: Wiley.

Emmanuel, Arghiri (1982). *Appropriate or Underdeveloped Technology?* New York: Wiley.

England, G. W. (1975). *The Manager and His Values: An International Perspective from the U.S., Japan, Korea, India, and Australia*. Cambridge, MA: Ballinger.

Ferrell, O. C., and John Fraedrich (1991). *Business Ethics, Ethical Decision Making and Ethics*. Boston: Houghton Mifflin.

Ferrell, O. C., and Larry G. Gresham (1985). "A Contingency Framework and Understanding Ethical Decision Making in Marketing." *Journal of Marketing* 49 (Summer), pp. 87–96.

Ferrell, O. C., and K. Mark Weaver (1978). "Ethical Beliefs of Marketing Managers." *Journal of Marketing* 42 (July), pp. 69–73.

FHG (1988). *Fraunhoffer-Gesellschaft, Annual Report*, English Summary. Munich, Germany: FHG.

Frame, J. Davidson (1983). *International Business and Global Technology*. Lexington, MA: Lexington Books.

Frank, Robert H., and Richard T. Freeman (1987). *Distributional Consequences of Direct Foreign Investment*. New York: Academic Press.

Fransman, M. (1990). *The Market and Beyond: Cooperation and Competition in Information Technology in the Japanese System*. Cambridge, England: Cambridge University Press.

Gaynor, Gerald H. (1991). *Achieving Competitive Edge through Integrated Tech Management*. New York: McGraw-Hill.

Ghosh, Pradip, ed. (1984). *Multinational Corporations and Third World Development*. New York: Greenwich Press.

Gibney, F. (1983). "Japan's Economic Secret." *Encyclopedia Britannica Book of the Year*, p. 465.

Goodman, Peter S. (1993). "Slavery: Plain and Simple." *The Progressive* 57 (June), pp. 26–28.

Goolsby, Jerry R., and Shelby D. Hunt (1992). "Cognitive Moral Development and Marketing." *Journal of Marketing* 56 (January), pp. 55–68.

Goulet, Denis (1977). *The Uncertain Promises—Value Conflicts in Technology Transfer*. New York: IDOC/North America, Inc.

Greenberger, Leonard S. (1992). "Senators Introduce Tech-Transfer Bill." *Public Utilities Fortnightly* 130, no. 2, pp. 40–41.

Hawkins, R. G., ed. (1979). *The Economic Effects of Multinational Corporations*. Greenwich, CT: JAI Press.

Heenan, David A. (1983). *The Re-United States of America: An Action Agenda for Improving Business, Government and Labor Relations*. Reading, MA: Addison-Wesley.

———— (1993). "China on the Move." *Journal of Business Strategy* 15 (May/June), pp. 35–40.

House, Karen Elliott (1995). "Two Asian Giants, Growing Apart." *Wall Street Journal*, February 24, p. 10.

Hunt, Shelby D., and Scott Vitell (1986). "A General Theory of Marketing Ethics." *Journal of Macromarketing* (Spring), pp. 5–16.

Hymer, Stephen (1972). "The Multinational Corporation and the Law of Uneven Development," in Jagdish Bhaghwati, ed., *Economics and World Order from 1970s to 1990s*. New York: The Macmillan Company.

Jain, O. P., and S. K. Savara (1981). *Industrialization and Multinationals*. Commercial Publications Bureau.

Jenkins, Rhys (1991). "The Impact of Foreign Direct Investment on Less Developed Countries: Cross-Section Analysis versus Industry Studies," in Buckley and Clegg, eds., *Multinational Enterprises in Less Developed Countries*. New York: St. Martin's Press.

Jo, Sung-Hwan (1979). "The Impact of Multinational Firms on Employment and Incomes: The Case Study of South Korea." ILO World Development Programme. Working Paper No. 12.

Kahler, Ruel (1983). *International Marketing*, 5th ed. Cincinnati: South-Western Publishing Co.

Keller, Bill (1994). "Corporate Foe of Apartheid Finds Reward Elusive." *New York Times*, December 9, p. A-4.

Kindleberger, C., and P. Audretsch, eds. (1983). *The Multinational Corporation in the 1980's*. Cambridge, MA: MIT Press.

Kindleberger, Charles, ed. (1970). *The International Corporation*. Cambridge, MA: MIT Press.

Kolde, Endel-Jacob (1982). *Environment of International Business*. Boston: Kent Publishing Company.

Kotler, Philip (1991). *Marketing Management: Analysis, Planning, Implementation, and Control*, 7th ed. Englewood Cliffs, NJ: Prentice-Hall.

Laczniak, Gene R., and Patrick E. Murphy (1991). "Fostering Ethical Marketing Decisions." *Journal of Business Research* 28, pp. 175–189.

Ladman, Jerry R. (1977). "Technology Transfer to Less Developed Countries." *Arizona Business* 24, no. 8 (October), pp. 15–21.

Lall, J., and M. Streeten (1977). *Foreign Investment, Transnationals and Developing Countries*. New York: The MacMillan Press, Ltd.

Leff, Nathaniel H. (1979). "Technology Transfer and U.S. Foreign Policy: The Developing Countries." *Orbis* (Spring), pp. 17–21.

Lizhi, Fang, and Zao Haiching (1994). "How to Boost China's Free Market—and Punish the State." *New York Times*, April 17, pp. 143, A27.

Lowenstein, Roger (1991). "U.S. Firms Move to Countertrading." *Wall Street Journal*, November 4, p. 22.

MacDougall, G. D. A. (1960). "The Benefits and Costs of Private Investment from Abroad: A Theoretical Approach." *Economic Record* 12 (September), pp. 23–45.

Madden, C. H., ed. (1977). *The Case for the Multinational Corporation: Six Scholarly Views*. New York: Praeger.

Mansfield, Edwin (1974). "Technology and Technological Change," in John H. Dunning, ed. *The Multinational Enterprise*. London: George Allen & Unwin, Ltd.

Martin, Christopher, Richard Lancionni, and John Gattorna (1985). "Managing International Customer Service," in Subash C. Jain and Lewis Tucker, Jr., eds., *International Marketing: Managerial Perspectives*. Boston: Kent Publishing Company, pp. 355–362.

Martin, Everette G., and Thomas E. Ricks (1985). "Selling Tool: Countertrading Grows as Cash-Short Nations Seeking Marketing Help." *Wall Street Journal*, March 16, p. 1.

Marton, Katherin, and Rana K. Singh (1991). "Technology Crisis for Third World Countries." *World Economy* 14, no. 2, pp. 199–213.

Mason, H. R. (1971). *The Transfer of Technology and the Factor Proportions Problem: The Philippines and Mexico*. Unitar Research Report 10.

——— (1973). "Some Observations on the Choice of Technology by Multinational Firms in Developing Countries." *Review of Economics and Statistics* 55, no. 3 (August), pp. 55–63.

Mason, Hal R. (1973). "The Multinational Firm and the Cost of Technology to the Developing Countries." *California Management Review* 15 (Summer), pp. 5–12.

McClelland, D. C. (1962). "Business Drive and National Achievement." *Harvard Business Review* 40, no. 4, pp. 99–112.

McClelland, D. C. et al. (1953). *The Achievement Motive*. New York: Appleton-Century-Crofts.

McClelland, D. C., and D. G. Winter (1969). *Motivating Economic Achievement*. New York: The Free Press.

McNulty, Sheila (1994). "West's Demand for Power Rangers Taxes Thai Factories." *Tallahassee Democrat*, December 17, p. 16A.

Merhav, Meier (1969). *Technological Dependence, Monopoly and Growth*. Exeter, England: Wheaton and Co.

Merryfield, Bruce D. (1983). "Forces of Change Affecting High Technology Industries." *National Journal*, January 29, p. 253.

Moffat, S. (1991). "Picking Japan's Research Brains." *Fortune*, March 25, pp. 84–96.

Monroe, Wilbur F. (1978). *Japanese Exports to the U.S.: Analysis of "Import Pull" and "Export Pull" Factors*. Washington, DC: U.S.-Japan Trade Council.

Morley, F., and J. Smith (1974). "The Choice of Technology: Multinational Firms in Brazil." Rice University Program in Development Studies. Paper no. 58 (mimeo).

Morse, Chandler (1975). "Making Science and Technology for Less Developed Countries." *Columbia Journal of World Business* (Spring), pp. 32–46.

The National Research Council (1977). *Appropriate Technologies for Developing Countries*. National Academy of Sciences.

Newfarmer, Richard (1980). *Transnational Conglomerates and the Economics of Dependent Development: A Case Study of the International Electrical Oligopoly and Brazil's Electrical Industry*. Greenwich, CT: JAI Press.

Norman, Henry R., and Patricia Blair (1982). "The Coming Growth in 'Appropriate' Technology." *Harvard Business Review* 60 (November–December), pp. 62–63, 66.

Office of Technology Assessment (1984). *Africa Tomorrow: Issues in Technology, Agriculture, and U.S. Foreign Aid*. Washington, DC: Congress of the United States.

Ohmae, Kenichi (1982). "The Secret of Strategic Management." *Management Review* (April), pp. 9–13.

Okoroafo, Sam C. (1993). "Firm Performance in Liberalized Environment: Empirical Evidence from a Developing Country." *Journal of Business Research* 28, pp. 175–189.

Ouchi, William (1981). *Theory Z: How American Business Can Meet the Japanese Challenge.* Reading, MA: Addison-Wesley.

Pacey, Arnold (1990). *Technology in World Civilization: A Thousand Year History.* Cambridge, MA: MIT Press.

Parry, Thomas G. (1980). *The Multinational Enterprise: International Investment and Host-Country Impacts.* Greenwich, CT: JAI Press.

Pascale, R. Tanner, and Anthony G. Athos (1981). *The Art of Japanese Management.* New York: Simon and Schuster.

Perlmutter, Howard V., and Tagi Sagafi-Nejad (1981). *International Technology Transfer: Codes, Guidelines and a Muffled Quadrilogue.* New York: Pergamon Press.

Peter, J. Paul, and James H. Donnelly, Jr. (1995). *Marketing Management Knowledge and Skills,* 4th ed. Chicago: Irwin.

Popper, Edward T., and Bruce D. Buskirk (1992). "Technology Life Cycles in Industrial Markets." *Industrial Marketing Management* 21, pp. 23–31.

Post, Tom, and Steven Strasser (1995). "No Free Lunches Here—China: A Survival Guide for Doing Business in the Middle Kingdom." *Newsweek* (February), pp. 29–40.

Rabino, S. (1980). "Examination of Barriers to Exporting Encountered by Small Manufacturing Companies." *Management International Review* 20, no. 1, pp. 67–73.

Racine, Philip J., and L. David Ford (1982). "Manufacturer–Overseas Distributor Relations and Export Performance." *Journal of International Business Studies* 13 (Fall), pp. 57–72.

Ramanwamy, V. S., and S. Namakumari (1990). *Marketing Management: Planning, Implementation, and Control—The Indian Context.* New Delhi, India: Macmillan India Ltd.

Ramesh, Jairam, and Charles Weiss, Jr., eds. (1979). *Mobilizing Technology for World Development.* New York: Praeger.

Rayner, Bruce C. P. (1989). "India Struggling to Enter the Electronics Age." *Electronic Business* 15, no. 1 (January 9), pp. 130–134.

Reddy, Allan C. (1991). "The Role of Marketing in the Economic Development of Eastern European Countries." *Journal of Applied Business Research* 7, no. 3, pp. 104–109.

——— (1994a). *Total Quality Marketing: The Key to Regaining Market Shares.* Westport, CT: Quorum Books.

——— (1994b). "International Franchising: Problems and Perspectives." Paper presented at 1994 Annual International Conference of the Association for Global Business, Las Vegas, NV, November 17–20.

Reddy, Allan C., Bruce D. Buskirk, C. P. Rao, and Niren M. Vyas (1994). "The Reciprocal Distribution Paradigm for Global Marketing." *Pan-Pacific Conference Proceedings,* Bangkok, Thailand, June 1–3, pp. 22–28.

Reddy, Allan C., and David Campbell (1994). *Marketing's Role in Economic Development.* Westport, CT: Quorum Books.

Reddy, Allan C., Jim Muncy, and Ajit Kaicker (1996). "Barriers to Technology Transfer." Paper presented at Global Conference on Small and Medium Industry and Business, Bangalore, India, January 3–5. Sponsored by SDM Institute for Management Development, Mysore, India and Indiana University-Purdue University, Fort Wayne, IN.

Reddy, Allan C., John E. Oliver, C. P. Rao, and A. L. Addington (1984). "A Macro-Behavioral Model of the Japanese Economic Miracle." *Akron Business and Economic Review* (Spring), pp. 41–49.

Reddy, Alan C., and C. P. Rao (1986). "Technology Transfer to Developing Countries: Problems and Perspectives." *International Issues* (Summer–Fall), pp. 7–12.

Reddy, Allan C., Beheruz N. Sethna, C. P. Rao, and Niren M. Vyas (1995). "Economic Prosperity through a Behavioral Growth Model: Developing Countries—India." Paper presented at "International Conference on Globalization and the Market Economy: The Challenges of Change," New Delhi, India, December 29–30.

Redwood, A. L. (1991). *Technology Transfer and University–Industry Liaison to Underpin Private Sector Innovation and Competitiveness in West Germany and the United Kingdom.* Report No. 184, Institute for Public Policy and Business Research, University of Kansas.

Rehder, R. R. (1981). "Japan's Synergistic Society: How It Works and Its Implications for the United States." *Management Review* 70, no. 10, pp. 64–70.

Reidenbach, Eric R., and Donald P. Robin (1988). "Some Initial Steps Toward Improving the Measurement of Ethical Evaluations of Marketing Activities." *Journal of Business Ethics* 7, no. 11, pp. 871–879.

Reuber, G. L. et al. (1973). *Private Foreign Investment in Development.* London: Oxford University Press.

Rhadu, G. M. (1973). "Some Aspects of Direct Foreign Investment in Pakistan." *Pakistan Development Review* (Spring), pp. 33–42.

Richman, Barry, and Melvyn Copen (1973). "Management Techniques in the Developing Nations." *Columbia Journal of World Business* 8 (Summer), pp. 49–58.

Robin, Donald P., and Eric R. Reidenbach (1987). "Social Responsibility, Ethics, and Marketing Strategy: Closing Gap Between Application and Practice." *Journal of Marketing* 51, no. 1, pp. 44–58.

Robock, Stefan H. J. (1980). *The International Technology Transfer Process.* Washington, DC: National Academy of Sciences.

Rogers, Everette M. (1962). *Diffusion of Innovations,* 3d ed. New York: Free Press.

Rogers, Everette M., and Floyd Shoemaker (1976). *Communications of Innovations: A Cross-Cultural Approach.* New York: Free Press.

Root, Franklin R. (1983). *Foreign Market Entry Strategies.* New York: AMACOM, a Division of American Management Association, Inc.

Rugman, Alan M., ed. (1983). *Multinationals and Technology Transfer—The Canadian Experience.* New York: Praeger.

Ryans, John K., and Lori Mitchell (1986). "The Changing Face of Foreign Trade." *Business Marketing* (January), pp. 49–67.

Saltz, Ira S. (1992). "Articulation and Economic Growth: Theory and Evidence." *Indian Journal of Economics* 72, no. 287 (April), pp. 22–35.

Saltz, Ira S., and R. J. Cebula (1993). "Capital-Intensity of Technology and the Presence of Foreign Direct Investment in the Third World: A Macroeconomic Approach." *Economia Internazionale* 46, no. 4, pp. 345–378.

Sanders, Christopher T. (1981). *East-West-South: Economic Interaction Between the Three Worlds.* London: Macmillan Press.

Saxenian, A. (1983). "The Genesis of Silicon Valley." *Britt Environment* 9, no. 1, pp. 7–17.

Scherer, F. (1992). "Competing for Competitive Advantage through Technological Innovation." *Business and the Contemporary World* 4, no. 3, pp. 17–33.

Schmid, R. D. (1991). " 'Biotechnology'—Related Research Associations in Japan." *Biotech Forum Europe* 8, pp. 166–170.

Sekiguchi, Sueo (1979). *Japanese Direct Foreign Investment, An Atlantic Institute Research.* New York: Allanhead, Osmun & Co.

Sen, A. K. (1960). *Choice of Technique.* London: Blackwell.

Sethi, S. Prakash (1993). "Operational Modes for Multinational Corporations in Post Aparthied South Africa: A Proposal for a Code of Affirmative Action in the Marketplace." *Journal of Business Ethics* 12, pp. 1–12.

Shelp, Ronald Kent, John C. Stephenson, Nancy Sherwood Truitt, and Bernard Wascow (1984). *Service Industries and Economic Development: Case Studies in Technology Transfer.* New York: Praeger.

Sheng, Piejua, Linda Chang, and Warren A. French (1994). "Business's Environmental Responsibility in Taiwan—Moral, Legal, or Negotiated." *Journal of Business Ethics* 13, no. 2, pp. 887–897.

Sigmund, Paul E. (1980). *Multinationals in Latin America.* Madison: University of Wisconsin Press.

Soundararajan, P. (1983). "Research Development and Transfer of Technology: Approach by the National Research Development Corporation of India." *Technovation* 2, no. 1 (February), pp. 55–60.

Stewart, Frances, and Paul Streeten (1971). "Conflicts Between Employment and Output Objectives in Developing Countries." *Oxford Economic Papers* 23, no. 2, pp. 67–81.

Stobaugh, Robert, and Louis T. Wells (1984). *Technology Crossing Borders.* Boston: Harvard University Press.

Stoffaes, C. (1984). "French Industrial Strategy in Sunrise Sectors," in Z. Griliches, ed., *R&D Patents and Productivity.* Chicago: University of Chicago Press.

Stone, Peter B. (1969). *Japan Surges Ahead.* New York: Praeger.

Streeten, Paul (1971). "Costs and Benefits of Multinational Enterprises in Less-Developed Countries," in John H. Dunning, ed., *The Multinational Enterprise.* London: George Allen & Unwin, Ltd.

Sturdivant, Frederick D., and James L. Ginter (1977). "Corporate Social Responsiveness: Management Attitudes and Economic Performance." *California Management Review* 19, no. 3, pp. 30–39.

Takeuchi, Kazuo (1982). *The Changing Work Ethic of the Japanese.* Special pamphlet published by Tokyo Economics University, No. 124.

Terpstra, Vern (1978). *The Cultural Environment of International Business.* Cincinnati: South-Western Publishing Co.

Thompson, Dennis (1982). "The UNCTAD Code on Transfer of Technology." *Journal of World Trade Law* (July–August), pp. 6–16.

Tsalikis, John, and David J. Fritzsche (1989). "Business Ethics: A Literature Review with a Focus on Marketing Ethics." *Journal of Business Ethics* 8, no. 9, pp. 695–744.

Ulrich, Peter, and Ulrich Thielmann (1993). "How Do Managers Think About Market Economies and Morality? Empirical Enquiries into Business-Ethical Thinking Patterns." *Journal of Business Ethics* 12 (November), pp. 879–898.

United Nations, Department of Economics and Social Affairs (1974). *Multinational Corporations in World Development*. New York: Praeger.

United Nations Group of Eminent Persons (1978). *Transnational Corporations in World Development: A Reexamination*. New York: United Nations.

Utrecht, Ernst (1978). *Transnational Corporations in South East Asia and the Pacific, vols. I & II*. Transnational Research Project, University of Sydney.

Vaitsos, Constantine (1974a). "Income Distribution and Welfare Considerations," in John H. Dunning, ed., *Economic Analysis and the Multinational Enterprise*. London: George Allen & Unwin, Ltd.

——— (1974b). *Intercountry Income Distribution and Transnational Enterprise*. London: Clarendon Press.

——— (1974c). "Employment Problems and Transnational Enterprises in Developing Countries: Distortions and Inequality." ILO World Employment Programme, Working Paper No. 11.

Varshney, R. L., and B. Bhattacharyya (1994). *International Marketing: An Indian Perspective*, 8th ed. New Delhi, India: Sultan Chand and Sons.

Verma, Y. S. (1980). "Marketing in Rural India." *Management International Review* 20, no. 4.

Vernon, Ray (1974). "The Economic Consequences of U.S. Foreign Direct Investment," in R. E. Baldwin and J. D. Robinson, eds., *International Trade and Finance*. Reading, MA: Little, Brown, and Company.

Vogel, Ezra F. (1978). "Guided Free Enterprise in Japan." *Harvard Business Review* (September–October), pp. 161–170.

——— (1979). *Japan As Number One: Lessons for America*. New York: Harper Colophon.

——— (1981). "The Miracle of Japan." *Saturday Review* 6, no. 11, pp. 18–23.

Vyas, N. M., J. Corey, and G. Hooker (1994). "From Russia with Love." *Machine Design* (February 21), pp. 8–12.

Vyas, N. M., J. Kauffman, and D. Rogers (1994). "Enhancing U.S. Competitiveness Through Technology Transfer from Federal Labs." Paper presented at "Competitiveness in the Global Marketplace Conference," Boston, MA.

Vyas, N. M., and J. H. Morehouse (1993). "Federal Technology Transfer." *Journal of Technology Transfer* 18, no. 182, pp. 91–94.

Vyas, N. M., and W. Shelburn (1992). "The Role of Marketing Faculty in the Technology Transfer Process." Paper presented at Western Marketing Educators Conference, Reno, NV.

Wadinambiatchi, George (1979). "Channels of Distribution in Developing Economies." *The Business Quarterly* (Winter), pp. 74–82.

Walsh, James I. (1985). "Mandated Countertrade: Implications for Global Marketing and Global Sourcing." *Issues in International Business* 2 (Summer), pp. 25–29.

Waugman, P. G. (1986). "Encouraging Innovation in North Carolina," in B. Gray, ed., *Technological Innovation Strategies for New Partnership*. Amsterdam, Netherlands: Elsevier.

Wells, L. T. (1973). "Economic Man and Engineering Man: Choice of Technology in a Low Wage Country." *Public Policy* 21, no. 3 (Summer), pp. 319–342.

Welt, Leo G. (1982). *Countertrade: Business Practices for Today's World*. New York: American Management Association.

Willmore, L. (1976). "Direct Foreign Investment in Central America Manufacturing." *World Development* 11, no. 8, pp. 51–59.

Author Index

Subject Index

About the Author

ALLAN C. REDDY is Professor of Marketing in the College of Business Administration, Valdosta (Georgia) State University. With more than 70 articles published in the academic journals and business media, Dr. Reddy's special expertise is in the field of economic growth and the uses of the behavioral approach. Among his books are two published by Quorum, *Total Quality Marketing: The Key to Regaining Market Shares* (1994) and *Marketing and Economic Development* (1993), with David Campbell.